MGA
RESTORATION GUIDE

By Malcolm Green

BROOKLANDS BOOKS

Published by

BROOKLANDS BOOKS

PO Box 146, Cobham, Surrey KT11 1LG, England
Phone: 01932 865051 Fax: 01932 868803

ISBN 1 85520 302 2
First published 1995

Printed and bound in Hong Kong

TABLE OF CONTENTS

ACKNOWLEDGEMENTS

I have always had tremendous enthusiasm and affection for the MGA and was delighted to find this was shared by the many people who have helped me with this book. It is surprising that people who make a living either working on the cars, or selling parts or services for them, manage to maintain this enthusiasm over the years, and I am very grateful that they were willing to assist me so much with the preparation of this guide.

As the title suggests, this is intended as a guide and not a replacement for the factory workshop manual and I suggest that anyone working on an MGA should have either an original copy, or one of the excellent reprints, in the workshop. In addition to the printed word, first hand help and advice is always useful and I would suggest this is best found by joining a club. In the United Kingdom the MGA Register and the Twin Cam Group, both part of the M.G. Car Club, offer technical help through publications and the periodic rebuild seminars.

I would like to take this opportunity to thank, in no special order, a few of the large number of people who helped me. Firstly Ken James (who was persuaded to stand the other side of the camera for a change) for posing, with his car, for the colour cover picture, and Gary Nicholls for allowing me to photograph many parts from his car.

The pushrod engine strip down and assembly was done by Gerry Brown of Merton Motorsport - in spite of the disruption I caused. As I have never owned or worked on a Twin Cam engine I had to rely heavily on Nick Cox and Peter Wood for the advice I have included. Peter Wood probably has had more years of involvement with these engines than anyone else. Brown and Gammons have a great deal of experience of MGAs and I must thank Ron, Valerie and Malcolm Gammons, and the helpful staff at Baldock, for putting up with me interrupting the smooth running of the workshop when taking pictures and asking questions.

Chris and Bruno Van Gestel of Anglo Parts and Jan van der Heijden (who does their bodywork) were most helpful when I visited them and I am also grateful for permission to use some of the drawings from their excellent parts catalogue. Richard and Vera Newton kindly gave me the chance to watch, and photograph, the assembly of an MGA seat at their company, Newton Commercial Ltd. John Marks of Vintage Restorations supplied me with the Smiths instrument information and I am grateful to Ashley Hinton for the details of the heater components. T & J Enterprises gave me much information on Lucas components.

For more than thirty years the world's leading motoring journals have allowed Brooklands Books to reissue their copyright material and I gratefully acknowledge their generosity in allowing the reproduction here of some of the remarks made in articles and road tests in those magazines as well as a couple of drawings. I am also grateful to the British Motor Industry Heritage Trust for the use of drawings from the workshop manuals.

CHAPTER ONE

INTRODUCTION

I like ALL M.G.s, and cannot think of any car built at Abingdon I would not wish to own, but since the day they were first announced to the public in September 1955 the MGA has always held a special place in my affections. As a teenager at that time, and living in what was then Southern Rhodesia, I was not able to actually drive one but well remember pestering our local B.M.C. agent for a catalogue as soon as cars started to appear in the country.

This is not the place to recount the story of the development of the MGA, or to give the history of M.G.s, as this has already been done by many better qualified than I to tell the tale. It is sufficient here to say that contrary to much I have seen written in recent years about the resistance of 'died in the wool' M.G. enthusiasts to the new car, my recollections, supported by press reports at the time, was that the overwhelming majority of enthusiasts welcomed a car that promised performance closer to that already enjoyed by drivers of Austin Healeys and Triumphs. No doubt there were complaints, but many of those were from people who owned one of the earlier cars, or those who had just bought a new TF and didn't like it suddenly looking way out of date!

As pre-publicity for the new model, these cars were entered for the 1955 Le Mans 24-Hour Race. Unfortunately as a publicity stunt this was not entirely successful as tooling-up problems delayed public announcement of the new model, and the dreadful accident there when so many spectators were killed when Levegh's Mercedes crashed into the crowd, dominated most of the reports of the race.

Nevertheless two of the M.G.s finished the race in 12th and 17th places. The third car, driven by Dick Jacobs, was involved in a very bad accident. MGAs were also entered in the Dundrod TT just prior to the public announcement of the car at the Frankfurt Motor Show.

The press had been given a preview of the car and "The Autocar", for example, had the chance to drive one of the Le Mans cars after it had been prepared for the Alpine Rally. They were very impressed with it and made no secret of the fact that they expected a production version to appear in due course - this must have made the sale of the last of those TFs even more difficult. They commented on the interest the car drew whenever it was parked and that it was obvious that the production version was eagerly awaited.

By September "The Autocar" team had been let loose on a production car and their road test was very favourable. Their opening comments made the point that the racing and record breaking activities of the M.G. Car Company had helped development of the cars and that, in essence, the differences between the Le Mans car they had tested earlier and the production car were small. They were impressed with the performance

An early press picture of the 1500. The M.G. Car Company often photographed cars in villages near Abingdon.

and recorded a best time to 70 mph of 21 seconds which they thought good with a full load on board. Interestingly the top speed with the hood and sidescreens in place was 99 mph, some three mph faster than the figure they recorded with just the optional low racing screen fitted and a tonneau cover over the passenger seat.

They also remarked in the report that the MGA seemed to be one of those cars whose cruising speed is determined by the road conditions and that where these were favourable it was possible to cruise for mile after mile at over 90 mph without the engine overheating. Those current owners of MGAs suffering from overheating should take note of this as it is evidence that there is no built-in design error that causes overheating and that problems with the car now are likely to result from a fault, or faults, introduced when the car was restored.

When the American "Road and Track" magazine were given a car to test they were equally impressed and particularly compared the performance with the superseded TF. They were surprised by just how well the car went and they recorded an increase in top speed of over 10 mph over that of the TF, with the cars weighing almost the same and power outputs of their engines likewise almost identical.

They attributed this increase to the lower drag body and the better gearing. They recorded a reduction in drag of 21% at 60 mph - quite a saving and a vindication of the radically new body styling adopted for the MGA.

The "Motor" magazine also published a road test of the new car in September in which they erroneously said that the aluminium skinned doors, boot and bonnet were only fitted to the pre-production cars - in fact they were present on every MGA! One point they did make was that the roadholding was improved by increasing the pressures of the standard crossply tyres above even the recommended figure for fast driving and that this increased pressure didn't make the car any more uncomfortable to travel in. From personal experience of an MGA still wearing its original tyres I can say that some increase in pressure over the recommended figure is necessary if the tyres are not to squeal on even very gentle bends.

The "Motor" road test was rather more detailed and searching than that carried out by "The Autocar" and the gearing ratios, particularly the low second gear, drew some criticism. They also did not much like the markings on the speedometer and rev. counter and it is perhaps significant that these were later changed to the style of instrument that remained current right up to the end of production of the MGB in 1980. However, they concluded their test by saying that the MGA could be "summed up as enthusiastically as it was everywhere received. That the modern styling is generally approved there can be no doubt, but far more important is the introduction of a small car with a degree of roadworthiness high by any standards. The famous slogan (Safety Fast!) of the factory has indeed never been better applied."

There is no doubt when reading contemporary reports of the enthusiasm for the new model. I can well remember the excitement at our school when one of the masters disposed of his Riley in favour of a bright red MGA and the only pity was that I had to wait four years before I was old enough to be able to drive one. There was certainly little feeling at the time that M.G. were in danger of loosing their traditional sports car buyer with

Rear view of the same early 1500. The car is fitted with the optional luggage rack essential for long distance touring.

This press picture is marked with an embargo until 22nd September 1955 and is thus of one of the early pre-production cars. What can be seen is the neat line of the wing piping - something very difficult to achieve.

the new model - merely as to whether they would be able to keep up with the demand from customers.

During 1956 the factory started listing a hardtop as an optional extra. The sidescreens supplied with this top were the more convenient sliding type but purchasers of the standard car still had to endure the earlier sidescreen with flaps designed to neatly remove gloves from the hand when fumbling to reach for the cable door release.

For the closed car enthusiast the company started building a very pretty coupe from September 1956. The Coupe had completely redesigned doors with external door handles and locks (on passenger's side only on early RHD. cars!) and winding windows. Along with the comfort of the fixed and lined roof came a differently trimmed and more luxurious interior;

although The "Motor" in August 1957 did criticise the lowness of the seats for the shorter driver and the fact that on wet but warm days the cockpit became a bit warm, but that rain came in if the windows or quarterlights were opened. However, overall they were full of praise for the car and said that it was no surprise that the MGA was then the world's most popular sports car.

The addition of the coupe roof and the modified doors surprisingly only added 32lbs to the weight of the car and the testers found that the smoother shape raised the top speed to over 100 mph and improved the fuel consumption. They remarked that anyone contemplating serious touring with the car would need the optional luggage rack for the boot and even today quite a high proportion of coupes seem to be equipped with them.

The neat hood stowage and the pocket for the sidescreens was an attractive feature of the MGA. The later 1600s and 1600 Mk IIs had a revised hood frame that allowed the sidescreens to stow further under the rear deck, rather than between the seats and bulkhead, which gave the seats more rearward travel.

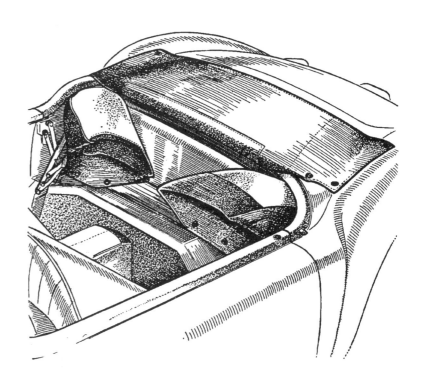

The B.M.C. stand at a car show in Florida. Sales of the cars in the U.S.A. brought much needed dollars to Britain.

The very pretty 1500 coupe. It is a pity that these cars do not seem to be as highly regarded as the roadsters with the result that they fetch lower prices on the classic car market and restoration of "basket cases" is less viable.

From the inception of the MGA the development department at Abingdon had been working on a higher performance model and prototypes of two different versions of twin overhead camshaft 'B' series engines had been tested and raced. Record breaking attempts at Utah with EX181 fitted with a very powerful twin OHC 1500cc engine showed the way and it was no surprise when the MGA Twin Cam was announced as a production car in 1958. With the standard car selling well there would appear to be no reason to add an additional model, but there is no doubt that at that time the management of the company, under the sure hand of John Thornley, was very much in favour of the competitive image the publicity for the new model created. I suppose, looked at in the light of cold figures, little profit must have been made on the sale of the Twin Cam - produced as it was in comparatively small numbers. However, the idea was probably to gain extra publicity for the marque to boost the sales of the standard cars.

The modifications for the new model were mostly mechanical, with the body appearing almost unchanged, but as we shall see even the body of the performance version differed from the standard car in some important

respects although some of the changes were later carried over into the 'cooking' model.

The earlier engines ran on a 9.9/1 compression ratio, although this was later reduced after a number of cases of piston failure occurred. The capacity of the engine was raised for the new model to 1588cc by increasing the cylinder bore. (this increased size neatly brought the car into the 1600cc class for international racing). The cross-flow cylinder head was aluminium and was fed by twin H6 carburettors. The chain drive for the overhead camshafts was covered by a large aluminium cover. The increased bulk of the engine meant that the radiator was mounted further forward and the header tank was mounted at the side of the engine, bolted to the manifold studs. A later modification was the addition of a pressure relief valve mounted separate from, and above, this header tank. An efficient extractor exhaust manifold and larger exhaust pipe helped them boost the power of the engine to around 107 bhp. Later changes to the compression ratio and the timing reduced this somewhat and the final version produced 100 bhp .

Along with the increase in engine power, without any change in overall gearing, went an improvement in

First production Twin Cam, PMO 326 - chassis YD1/501, fitted with the competition seats (above). Contrast with the later series car (below), which also has competition seats but features the 1600 style lights.

stopping ability. Dunlop disc brakes were fitted on all four wheels allied to peg driven, centre lock Dunlop disc wheels. These wheels, with the discrete 'Twin Cam' badges fixed either side of the bonnet and on the boot lid were the only external distinguishing features of the higher performance model.

In the cockpit thicker seats could be fitted as an optional extra and these were ordered on many of the cars built. These seats were never listed as basic equipment, just as extras, and they could also be ordered fitted to the standard MGA 1600s. Although billed as more comfortable these seats do have one noticeable drawback for the taller driver; they substantially reduce the leg room as the seat backs are much thicker. To add to the feeling of more luxury the dashboard was covered with a leather grained cloth to match the upholstery.

The car was enthusiastically received by the press at the launch, held at the Defence Department's banked test track at Chobham in Surrey, many prominent motoring journalists of the time had plenty of opportunity to try out the performance for themselves. The shortcomings of the design - one of which was excessive oil consumption on some cars - tended to be played down in the enthusiasm over the performance but to their credit the magazines did emphasise the special nature of the model and that it was intended primarily for the competition orientated owner. There is no doubting the extra performance available, quite remarkable for a 1600cc car at the the time with "The Autocar" recording a maximum speed of 114 mph, and a Twin Cam was the first car I was driven in at over 100 mph! However, the heavy oil consumption of the earlier cars (five pints needed on one 800 mile journey by "The Autocar") meant that a factory modification to the piston rings was urgently undertaken.

The service record at first was poor as many owners, especially abroad, did not appreciate the special requirements of the tuned engine for good fuel and careful ignition timing, it was not until the compression ratio was lowered, and the distributor modified to prevent over advance of the spark, that acceptable reliability was gained.

The poor reliability of some of these earlier cars, plus the improvements made to the standard cars with the introduction of the 1600 in 1959, eventually led to the abandonment of production after just over 2,000 examples had been built. However, I do not see the car

as a failure but rather as a special model that added to the performance image of the marque in general and must have helped overall sales of the cars. Today there are many enthusiastic owners of these cars who swear by their reliability - if not their accessibility for routine service.

By 1959 it became apparent that to keep up with the competition some changes to the MGA would be needed. To help improve sales the MGA 1600 was announced with the engine capacity increased to 1588cc - the same as the Twin Cam - by the same expedient, that is by increasing the bore from 73.025 mm to 75.39 mm. This raised the power by 7.5 bhp and the torque by about 12% which, as the gearing and axle ratio was unaltered, made quite a noticeable difference to the acceleration times. In "The Autocar" road test the car managed to reduce the 0 - 60 mph time to 14.2 secs. whilst the "Motor" team managed an even more creditable 13.3 secs. The top speed reached by "The Autocar" was 101.4 mph with the rival magazine only managing 100 mph. In any event the new car was now a true 100 mph machine.

Along with the engine modifications was an improvement to the brakes. The front brakes were now discs but of Lockheed design, rather than Dunlop as fitted to the Twin Cam. The rear brake linings were also changed. To compliment the mechanical changes the body was given 1600 badges front and rear and the rear light plinths were extended to incorporate separate amber flashers with the front sidelights enlarged to feature an amber segment. These alterations were needed to meet changing regulations outlawing the previous arrangement where a relay interrupted the brake light circuit to provide flashing turn indicators.

Some new colour schemes were adopted and the previously available black hood dropped in favour of grey, beige or light blue to tone with the exterior colour. The sidescreens were modified to incorporate sliding windows, similar to those fitted with a hard top, but the frames were fabric covered rather than aluminium.

The effect of these changes was to improve an already good car and to bring the specification more up to date - particularly in respect of the disc brakes which were then regarded as something most sports car drivers desired - much as ABS or 4-wheel drive is looked at now. The good sales of the 1600, allied to service difficulties with the Twin Cam, had the latter being

A 1600 coupe with disc wheels. I expect to upset a lot of people when I say I prefer these to wire wheels! The coupe is certainly a very attractive car from almost any angle and its smooth shape gave it a higher top speed.

The interior of the 1600 coupe. The seats were different from those fitted to the roadster and from the de luxe competition seats that could be specified for the Twin Cam and all 1600 coupes. The central arm rest did not have the pleats seen on roadsters, and was the same for both standard or competition seats. The carpets on all but the first few coupes were grey and the battery cover was carpeted, unlike the roadsters. The uncluttered area behind the seats on the 1600s can be compared with the 1500 interior seen opposite. The extra space was created by moving the spare wheel to a position completely within the boot. Replacing the headlining is one of the more difficult jobs.

The 1500 coupe rear shelf inside the window is much deeper than that fitted to the 1600. The spare wheel is stowed in the same position as it is on the roadster, leaving very little room behind the seats for luggage.

This very neat door handle replaces the rather crude internal cord pull used in the roadster.

The door locks and rear door pillars on the coupe are very different from those fitted to the roadster.

dropped from the range with the last car being built in April 1960 after which just one more car, a special order painted in Woodland Green, was built for Michael Ellman-Brown. He still has this car and it has yet to reach 10,000 miles.

For the last year of MGA production and whilst the development team were actually working flat out on its replacement - the MGB - some changes were made to the car to produce the 1600 Mk II. The most significant external changes were to the grill and tail lights. The grill was modified to recess the slats at the bottom - perhaps the opposite to a 'face lift'! This change does not do a great deal for the frontal appearance of the car but I cannot say, as some do, that it spoils the looks. At the rear the lights were moved inboard and Mini style units were substituted for the previous separate brake and flasher lamps, possibly to cut costs.

Internally the cockpit was much improved by the adoption of the Twin Cam style covered dashboard. The fabric covering of the top of the scuttle also included in the changes removed the previous criticism of the windscreen reflections on light coloured cars.

The most significant change, however, and the one that places this model top of my list of desirable MGAs, was to the engine and rear axle. The engine was enlarged from 1588 cc to 1622 cc - the size of engine soon to be used in other BMC 'B' engined models - and substantially redesigned internally. Changes to the width of the main bearings allowed for the crankshaft to have a sturdier and stiffer construction. The engine block was changed and equipped with re-designed

The distinctive centre-lock Dunlop disc wheels fitted to Twin Cam MGAs and to those pushrod cars with the optional disc brakes on all four wheels that were available from the start of 1600 production in 1959.

Only the 1600 Mk II was fitted with the recessed grill. This was to try to up-date the car to stimulate flagging sales in the face of increased competition from other marques. Actually it was the mechanical changes to the car that were of greater significance for owners.

pistons and con-rods. A lot of work had been carried out on the cylinder head with the combustion chambers being re-shaped and the sizes of the valves increased. The effect of those substantial changes was to raise the power to 90 bhp at 5,500 rpm which compares favourably with the output of the Twin Cam which produced around 107 bhp but at the much higher engine speed of 6,500 rpm. Add to this the fact that the later Twin Cams actually had less power (100 bhp at 8.3 : 1 compression) then you will see that in normal road driving, as opposed to racing, the 1600 Mk II was just about as fast as the Twin Cam and perhaps rather less temperamental. The acceleration of the Mk II was, however, masked slightly by another change made - that of reducing the rear axle ratio from 4.3 to 4.1 which made the car less fussy at higher speeds.

Comparison of road test figures with those for the earlier car do not show the last of the MGAs in quite as good a light as they should because of the change in gearing. In acceleration terms the newer car was only slightly faster. However, that was not the whole story and for my money the changes were significant and the new engine - originally destined for the MGB unchanged - before being enlarged to 1800cc at a later stage - is a superb unit. It is perhaps slightly less smooth than the 1500 but feels a lot more lively and, thanks partly to a lightened flywheel, a lot more responsive to the throttle.

Although soon to be replaced by the MGB the final version of the MGA is an improved car over the earlier types, which is just as it should be.

The disappearance of the Twin Cam from the range left the factory with a number of Twin Cam chassis and other components surplus and the marketing men offered the option of the Twin Cam goodies - disc brakes, competition seats, etc. - on the pushrod cars. Some of the 1600 Mk IIs were actually designated as 'de-luxe' models when fitted with these extras. Most of these special models seem to have been sold on the export market - possibly to help boost flagging sales of a car that was by now looking slightly out of date. The arrival of such cars as the Sunbeam Alpine and offerings from continental competitors like Alfa-Romeo, all with luxuries like winding windows and roomier cockpits, meant that the writing was on the wall for the MGA and a replacement, the MGB, was needed.

Nevertheless it is fortunate for enthusiasts, such as us, that over 100,000 of these superb driver's cars had been built before production ended and that, unlike the later MGB, these were all built before legislation had forced any design changes that would have spoilt the original purity of the shape - imagine an MGA with the rubber impact-absorbing bumpers foisted on the poor MGB.

The last version of the MGA roadster, the 1600 Mk II. The rear lights are the same as those fitted to the Mini.

TWIN CAM AND DE-LUXE MODELS

The body of the Twin Cam differed from that used on the pushrod cars in a number of important areas. Starting from the front, the duct panel behind the grill is noticeably shorter than on the standard cars as the radiator is mounted further forward to clear the bulkier engine. From chassis 592 (roadster) and 594 (coupe) access panels were provided under the front wheel arches. The bonnet (hood) was modified to clear the higher engine and the bonnet prop was moved to the left hand side of the car. The modified bonnet was later used on the 1600 and 1600 Mk II.

The hole in the bulkhead for the heater box is nearer the right hand side of the car, and the spacing of the nine holes for the bolts that fix the bulkhead to the chassis crossmember varies from the standard car to accommodate the different pedal box used for the Dunlop brakes.

The spacing of the holes for the 'Twin Cam' badges on the sides of the bonnet (hood) and on the boot (trunk) lid are different to those for the '1600' and '1600 Mk II' badges.

The chassis was also modified and the front brackets for the steering rack were fixed further forward. The rack itself was changed for one with a longer pinion shaft. The greasing points for the rack were placed underneath it and not on top. After the first few cars were built the factory modified the front cross member, drilling five holes in it to allow access to the sump securing bolts.

The offside engine mountings and mounting brackets were different from the pushrod cars. The front springs were modified to compensate for the heavier engine and were slightly longer than the standard units. Once the second series - with 1600 style lights, etc. - was introduced the anti-roll bar was made a standard fitment.

The front hubs were fitted with taper roller bearings as used on early MGBs. The stub axle and hub were different and the brake calliper was the Dunlop type similar to that fitted to Jaguar Mk IIs. On later cars the bridge pipe was held with a 'P' clip to avoid brakages at the nipple due to fatigue.

The mounting bracket in the engine compartment for the starter solenoid was at a different angle. The rear axle case was the same as the standard wire wheeled cars but the ends of the tubes and the hubs were different.

The so called 'de-luxe' models that used up Twin Cam components vary in specification. Initially, apart from the engine, they were almost pure Twin Cam with the modified body, chassis, steering rack, brakes, etc., but towards the end of production they were closer to the pushrod cars with just the modified brakes and wheels fitted.

Early Twin Cam engine bay.

CHANGES IN PRODUCTION (from parts lists)

MGA 1500 Nos. 10101 - 68850

10501   Changes made to hood, frame and sidescreens.
10917 (disc wheel) 11450 (wire wheel). The hub nuts fixing hub to axle casing changed to accommodate handed nuts.
12800   Modified wiper blades and arms for LHD cars (RHD cars had the same modification from chassis 13612).
13473   Modified wiring harness introduced.
14090   Instruments changed from earlier style with numbers in 20 mph increments to those with numbers in 10 mph increments.
15152   Coil springs modified.
17588   Speedometer and rev. counter cables modified.
19949   Sill finishers to cover lower fixing bolts introduced. These are often omitted from restored cars.
20162   Hood modified with rear quarter windows added to improve vision.
20753   Prop shaft changed.
27989 (disc wheel) 28540 (wire wheel) Threads on brake and clutch pipe fittings changed from BSP to UNF.
29935   Splash panel added to front of rear wings of roadster.
42613   Improved insulation spacer for carburettors together with gaskets (four per car).
45186   Modified windscreen washer push and jets fitted.
48730   Wheel knock-ons on wire wheel cars lose the 'M.G.' octagon symbol.
54247   Front suspension steering knuckles and arms modified. (Substitute later items for earlier only in sets).
57100   Strengthened windscreen pegs in steel instead of brass fitted. (Service MG/232).
57574   LHD cars (except North America) temperature gauge calibrated in centigrade instead of Fahrenheit.
58713   Brake pedal modified. Clutch pedal on LHD cars modified.
58918   Headlamps for LHD cars changed to vertical dip units (French market cars from 60340).
60632 (RHD) 60637 (LHD). Tonneau cover modified and fastenings on doors deleted. Later covers did not have pocket sewn in for steering wheel.
61100   RHD cars had modified clutch pedal.
61160   Heater water valve changed.
61504   15GD engine introduced necessitating longer speedometer cable (5ft 6in instead of 5ft 3in) on LHD

cars. The toe board and carpet on RH side of cockpit modified to accommodate high mounted starter. Propeller shaft modified.
63435   Cable and connections between starter switch and motor modified.
63577   Modified stronger disc wheels fitted. Deeper dishing of centre gives greater clearance for the disc brakes fitted later to the 1600.
66574   Chassis extensions and spring pans modified to allow for fitting of an anti-roll bar. (These later extensions can be fitted to earlier cars to facilitate fitting an anti-roll bar.)

MGA 1600 nos. 68851 - 100351

69505   Disc to hub studs replaced by bolts on disc wheel cars.
70276   Modified hubs fitted and studs replaced with bolts (wire wheel cars).
71832   Radiator cap with higher (7 lbs) pressure fitted (modified again from 88192).
74979   Speedometer cable on RHD cars changed.
78249   To counter claims of insufficient rearward seat adjustment the hood frame was modified to stow it farther back under the rear deck. The stowage bag for the sidescreens was also modified so they stowed higher up and not between the seat and the rear battery compartment.
80384   Modified windscreen wiper wheel boxes fitted.
80390   Windscreen washer pump and bottle changed. Bottle neck diameter increased from 1.5in to 2.2in.
82749 (wire wheel) 88893 (disc wheel). Differential and half shafts modified from 10 spline to 25 spline.
91240   From this point the 1600 de-luxe was introduced as an option with Dunlop disc brakes all round and centre lock disc wheels.
96269 (grey hood) 96806 (beige hood) 97104 (blue hood). Sidescreens modified.

MGA 1600 Mk II nos. 100352 - 109070

100612   Fuel pump changed from S.U. AUA54 to AUA154.
101292   On roadsters the rear door pillar finishers were modified to improve water sealing.
101352   Gasket for rear lamps changed from black rubber to white 'Prestik', 1/2in wide, 1/8in thick.
102381   Modified distance pieces fitted to rear bumper mountings.

102589 (disc wheels) 102929 (wire wheels) Dust shields fitted to front disc brakes on Lockheed braked cars.

103261 (disc wheels) 103834 (wire wheels) Modified disc brake calliper dust seal introduced.

Twin Cam nos. 501 - 2192 (1500 style body) 2193 - 2611 (1600 style body)

592 (roadster) 594 (coupe) Access panels fitted in wheel arches to facilitate access to service items.

652 (also 575, 613, 623, 633 and 648) New 7 lb. relief valve fitted to radiator overflow and plain filler cap fitted to header tank - service sheet MG/234.

713 LHD cars fitted with longer speedometer cable. (5ft 6in instead of 5ft 3in)

836 (approx.) Disc brake callipers modified .

994 Tonneau cover changed and fasteners deleted from tops of doors.

997 Master cylinder box and mounting plate modified.

1840 (approx.) Rear hub extensions modified.

2275 Chassis front extensions modified to accommodate anti-roll car (now standard).

2371 Half shafts modified.

2467 Modified speedometer cable for RHD cars.

2468 Air cleaners modified.

2540 To provide more rearward seat adjustment the hood frame was modified to stow farther back under the rear deck. The stowage bag for the sidescreens was also changed so they stowed higher up and not between the seat and the rear battery compartment.

2544 Windscreen washer pump and bottle changed. Bottle neck diameter increased from 1.5in. to 2.2in.

2545 Modified windscreen wiper wheel boxes fitted.

'Er...George, I think I've made a mistake'

CHAPTER TWO

BUYING AND RESTORING AN MGA

Going out and looking for a car to purchase, once having decided to buy an MGA, should be a pleasurable experience. However, as in most things, there will be times when it will seem to be not such a good idea and inevitably cars will turn out to be entirely different when viewed to the description given in advertisements, or by the vendor over the telephone. Often one wonders if they have been talking about the same car!

To make things easier it is better to work to some sort of plan. It is obviously a waste of time viewing restoration projects, just because they are cheap, if a good, sound, running car is what is wanted. Likewise it is a waste of money buying a car that has been superficially 'restored' by a trader merely to increase its price if it is intended to strip down and carry out a chassis up rebuild anyhow.

So let's get down to basics. Firstly is it certain than an MGA will fit your needs? Have you driven one? Does it have enough room? Too many people have bought non-running cars and spent small fortunes working on them only to find that they don't like driving the finished vehicle. There are plenty of enthusiastic owners around who would be only too happy to take you for a drive in their cars and may even be persuaded to allow you a turn at the wheel - insurance company willing.

Secondly is a particular model required? If a 1600

coupe is really wanted then it is a waste of time looking at a 1500 roadster 'just to see'. At best just the time will be wasted. At worst you might talk yourself, or be persuaded, into buying the thing and then wish for ever after that you had stuck out for the car you really wanted.

Thirdly, find out as much as you can about MGAs before buying one. You really need to know which models had which features originally and what a correct car should look like. The information contained within these covers will give a purchaser most of the information needed to separate a good car from a bad one.

Once the choice has been narrowed down to a particular model, or price, then the hunt through the advertisements can start. When looking for a car at the lower end of the price range it is as well to have some idea of how much it will cost to have any faults rectified or parts replaced. When looking at cars requiring full restoration remember that, at present, it would be unlikely that anything like the full cost of such a restoration could be recovered when the car is sold, particularly if much of the work is done professionally. However careful one is, costs will escalate and the final bill is likely to well exceed the market value of the car. For this reason unless the actual job of carrying out the restoration work appeals it may be better to look out for a car that only needs a little work, although the initial cost may be higher, but as I have said before beware of the car that looks superficially good but will in the end need a full rebuild.

So, armed with all the information needed, an expedition to look at a suitable car is contemplated; but what should one look for when faced with the vehicle? The first and most important rule is not to be in a hurry. Do not buy a car without examining it in a good light and, if possible, in good weather. Do not even bother to look at a car that the vendor does not make accessible for inspection. Cars hidden at the back of garages under piles of junk are probably in even worse condition in the inaccessible areas than the visible parts.

When looking at a car that has been dismantled extra care must be taken to ensure that all the parts are there and that they are correct for the car. As a general rule if the car has parts for more than one vehicle with it - or if there appear to be other MGA parts around - then it is possible that what is offered for sale is an assembly of parts from lots of different cars. Often these will be bits rejected by the vendor when he was working on another car and he knows he will probably not be able to sell them separately for as much as he can get for a 'complete' car. From experience I can say that this sort of project should only be taken on in the full knowledge that many of the parts with the car will prove to be either incorrect for the model and year or need replacing for some other reason.

EXAMINING THE CAR

Go prepared with suitable clothing and perhaps some ramps if an underbody inspection is contemplated. I would also suggest, perhaps, a torch and screwdriver. If the vendor has indicated that he is prepared for you to drive the car then find out from your insurance company whether they will cover you. Most policies will only cover damage caused by the policyholder to other cars and other third party risks but do not cover the car being driven unless they are first notified. However, just trying the car in the driveway limiting this to checking the controls, instruments and so on may be sufficient when allied to a ride in the passenger seat with the vendor at the wheel. Actually a ride like this will give some idea of the condition of the car and the driver can always be asked to demonstrate the brakes or accelerate up a hill if this helps. There will also be no worry about damaging the car and then feeling obliged to buy it anyway, or coping with possibly unfamiliar roads.

When first looking at the car ignore the sales patter from the owner and take a good look round it and at its general condition. If the car sought needs to be perfect and the one on offer does not rate that description perhaps now is the time to walk away from the deal. The more time is spent examining the car, and the longer the vendor has to work on you, the more chance there is of starting to sell the car to yourself. I know this may sound a bit silly, but it is all too easy to start to gloss over the faults and shortcomings and start thinking about rectifying those faults. DON'T DO IT! If the first impression of the car was that is wasn't right - LEAVE IT THERE.

Having decided to look more closely, now is the time to take a more careful look at the outside. Check the car sits square and that, looking down the sides, there are no ugly ripples. Look at the joins at the front of the shroud and the front wings - do they line up? Look at the back panel and the rear wings - does the lower edge line up? Do the door gaps look right and do the doors, especially at the lower rear edge, line up with the bodywork correctly? Are there all the correct join lines in the sills or have the sills been plated over or bodged with filler? On later cars is the strip that covers the lower fixing bolts on the wing still in place?

Now the doors and door pillars must be carefully examined. On the MGA this is a weak area and also one where poor repairs are often made. Check the fit of the doors, do they open and close well? Try pushing down the doors with them open to see if the front pillar is sound. Look at the lock area and at the paint for signs of a sagging door rubbing it away. Whilst by the doors, feel underneath the sills, between them and the chassis, to see if the inner sills are still whole. If, later on, an underbody inspection is carried out then take a closer look here. Look at the cappings on the door and body to see that they line up.

Open the boot (trunk) lid and look for rust on the floor and on the rear panel. Repair panels, and even a complete floor, are available but replacement is difficult and expensive. Whilst here look at the spare wheel and tools just so you know they are there!

Open the bonnet (hood) and look at the inner wings and bulkhead and particularly at the chassis rails and the bracing strut to the scuttle. Frontal impact or a blow forcing the wheel against the chassis can cause damage here. Damage to the front duct panel is common on

MGAs where the front has had a knock. If the car is a Twin Cam, or one of the de-luxe models, note the body differences listed elsewhere. Whilst at the front of the car look at the grill to see how well it fits. Is the piping in place and is it firmly held by the grill? Many replacement grills are a poor fit and as we will see later when looking at repairing bodies care is needed to make them fit properly.

On the subject of replacement parts I must make a comment here about bumpers. There have been some reproduction MGA bumpers sold that are, frankly, just rubbish. The shapes are all wrong and it is very difficult to make them look right. Unfortunately the original items are often damaged, particularly the front, but these should always be retained if possible. Dents can be knocked out and extra holes can be filled before re-chroming but if they are very badly rusted then either better secondhand parts, or replacements, will be needed. The new parts now available are a lot better than some earlier efforts, although by no means perfect, and some of those offered by some suppliers are better than those sold by others .

THE MECHANICAL COMPONENTS.

With an MGA the mechanical condition of the car is, perhaps, less important than the condition of the chassis and body. However, having said that, it is important that all the correct components are present. It is no good paying top price for a car that later turns out to have been fitted with the wrong engine and a lot of non-original smaller components. If paying top price for a car, then the mechanical condition should reflect this.

U.S. tennis champion, Darlene Hard, bought this MGA 1600 from University Motors in 1960. The car has been fitted with a number of extras such as map reading lights, additional calibrated speedometer and tripmeter and stop watch. Obviously the car was going to be used for rallying and the top surface of the scuttle has been covered in a dark fabric to reduce reflections in the windscreen - as was later done on all 1600 Mk II models.

A lot of cars are now sold has having 'matching numbers'. This usually means that the numbers appearing on the engine, gearbox and back axle match the log book or the original build details. However, this may only mean that the restorer has applied new engine plates and so on to match the details he has for the car!

If possible the engine should be run for quite a while when any unwelcome noises should become apparent. After a test drive or ride, preferably getting the engine thoroughly hot, leave it running for a while. An engine in poor condition will soon exhibit signs of oil smoke from the rocker cover cap and erratic idling. The hot oil will not easily disguise worn bearings and oil pressure may be low. There should be no signs of overheating at idle and if the temperature gauge climbs rapidly then there are some problems present. The idle on a 1500 or 1600 should be even at about 800 rpm but on the Mk II and the Twin Cam it may be a little more uneven on some cars without necessarily indicating an out of tune engine. I have also found a greater tendency for the Mk II engine to 'run on' after being switched off.

The test drive should also have indicated the condition of the gearbox and back axle, especially if the hood (soft top) was up. Suddenly lifting the throttle in the lower gears will show up any tendency to jump out of gear and any excessive noise in the gearbox and back axle indicates problems. Whilst on the drive note the instruments. Do the rev counter and speedometer work and are the speed and revolutions indicated correct for the car? Some cars have rebuilt instruments, or replacements, that are wrongly geared.

When MGA chassis are badly rusted then they can be very weak indeed. In this example the inner face of the side rail has completely disappeared alongside where the floorboards were fitted. Moisture between the boards and the side of the chassis has rotted it away and water getting through the gap has settled in the bottom of the box section damaging this as well.

The same chassis but this time at the front of the passenger footwell. Here again, most of the damage has come from sodden floorboards. The inner chassis rail will have to be replaced and new floorboard supports fitted.

After a run it is time to look underneath for any signs of oil leaks. Any substantial leaks from the bell housing could indicate a worn oil seal at the back of the engine. Rectification of this is neither simple nor cheap. If the housing on the rear bearing cap in the block, as well as the scroll on the crankshaft are worn then the only remedy is to have the housing built up and re-machined - or look for another block.

The condition of the chassis is vitally important. It must be sound, free of rust and straight. Obviously a cheap car that requires a full rebuild will be judged by different standards but do not underestimate the amount of work required to repair a badly rusted chassis. Because of the box section construction the actual amount of rusting present will always be a lot more than is at first apparent. The worst areas are the side members alongside the sills. This part usually receives no additional protection from oil leaks and is most vulnerable to blasting with road grit and the accumulation of wet mud between the sill and the chassis. Additionally some wadding was inserted inside the chassis at this point, to try to stop noise travelling along the rails from the engine compartment to the occupants, and this absorbs and holds moisture.

The floor boards should be examined from above and below. Replacement with ply is fairly straightforward but if moisture has collected here then the mounting strips and the adjacent chassis can suffer badly.

On this car the bottom of the rear door pillar, the inner and outer sills and some of the main chassis rail have rotted away. The cost of repairing all this damage will be considerable. A project like this should only be undertaken if most of the work can be done at home as the cost of having the car restored professionally would probably exceed its value when completed.

The floor and rear end of the boot (trunk) suffers badly where water has been leaking in. Complete floor panels are available - but expensive.

INTERIOR AND WEATHER EQUIPMENT.

The first look at the car would have given some idea of the condition of the interior but perhaps a closer look is needed now. Firstly, especially on a car from a hot climate, are the seats leather? Some plastic seat materials are good, and will not deteriorate so quickly in the sun, but non-originality here should be reflected in the price. Replacing the seat covers with leather is expensive.

It is usual for MGA seats to sag, especially if the original Dunlopillo foam is still in place, and new interiors for the seats can help here. However, if the leather is badly cracked then it will probably need replacing. Faded seats, or even those of the wrong colour, can be repainted with one of the special kits available for the purpose or given to a specialist for attention. I have never used these materials, having always elected to recover - or replace entirely - worn out seats, but some of the results of the process I have seen look good.

Look at the hood (soft top) to see its condition and especially whether the frame is undamaged. Often frames have been broken when a seized pivot has been forced. Remember the later cars had a different pattern frame. The sidescreen design changed with the 1600 but many cars, even early 1500's, have later gained the sliding pattern sidescreens which are a lot more convenient to use.

Well, having looked all round a decision is needed. Remember that unless you are sure the car is exactly right now is the time to decline to make an offer. It is better to take the time to look around at other cars than to buy something that may later prove to be an expensive mistake. If you have driven a good MGA you will know just what a nice car they are. They steer well, are comfortable and feel safe and secure - even in modern traffic. Should you join the many other MGA owners you will be sure to enjoy the experience. M.G. people are a friendly bunch!

When the MGA 1600 was announced in July 1959 much was made in press releases of the improved sidescreens. Here we see these, along with the hood which was now available in a new range of colours. Sliding sidescreens had previously only been available with a hard top and were aluminium framed - not fabric covered.

RESTORATION - GENERAL ADVICE.

Before buying a car to restore, or starting to take a good car to pieces, think carefully whether you have the necessary skills, time, money and patience to carry the job through. Most restorations take at least four times as long, and cost three times as much, as the original estimate. Many of the 'basket cases' started off as perfectly sound cars before being pulled apart by people with more enthusiasm than sense.

If buying a complete car in working order you could, perhaps, consider doing a running rebuild, working on just one section at a time. For example, one year rebuild the engine and then have some fun with the car before starting, say, on the bodywork the next year. In this manner the car can be slowly improved without having it off the road for years on end. Of course, there are some of us who are never happy until we have completely stripped the car down - to spend all our spare time for the next year or three in the garage. We are just as likely to sell the thing once finished and look for another heap to start pulling apart. There is a word somewhere for people like us......!

WORK TO A PLAN

If deciding on a complete rebuild then some sort of plan can help. You will have an idea how much work you can do yourself and how much you intend to leave to specialists. Approach these early on to get an idea of costs, and of the time scale they work to - then double it! If the car is complete, photograph every angle and talk to experts on the model to decide what is right and what is wrong with it. Take measurements and look at the fit of the wings, doors and so on. If anything is wrong then try to decide why. If, for example, a door does not fit then check to see if it is because of something simple, like the hinge position, or if the door pillar is incorrectly aligned. Try adjusting the fits before taking the car apart. It is no good expecting the car to fit back together after respraying it if any errors originally apparent are not corrected.

Take a good look at the runs of pipes, wiring, etc., take photographs and make notes and drawings. When the time comes to put the whole lot back together much of this detail will be forgotten - I have done so too often! It is certainly a good idea to always have a note pad available in the workshop to jot down notes and lists of parts needed as work progresses. Steam cleaning

before starting dismantling will make the job a bit easier - but remember that the whole car must be dried out immediately as the rust will form on the unprotected surfaces very quickly. Also remember that the steam will penetrate into many components through quite small apertures.

When starting to dismantle the car make sure all components are easily identifiable. I find a supply of those resealable plastic bags useful and usually keep all the fixing nuts and bolts with the appropriate components. Although they may not be used again they will indicate what size and type of fixing was used. In some cases the old nuts and bolts can be cleaned and replated if similar new items are unavailable. For example many items that originally may have had 'Phillips' heads are now only available with 'Posidrive' slots which will upset some purists.

Start lists of new parts needed and order these early. It is frustrating to have to wait at a later stage because something is temporarily out of stock. The only note of caution here is to stress that any new components should be examined carefully when purchased as it may be difficult to persuade a supplier to change a defective item many months, or years, later if the rebuild takes a long time.

Talking about time, although it is not always a good idea to work to a deadline, some sort of target may be preferable. If you do hand any part of the restoration to a specialist then it may help to give him a date to work to. In my experience the only one who gains in the sort of 'fit it in when you can' type of arrangement is the restorer. He will always work hardest for the person pressing him most for the job to be finished and will seldom reflect the patience of the customer prepared to wait in either the price or quality of the finished job.

Whilst setting targets it is quite nice, occasionally, to get something completely finished. Whether it be the engine rebuilt or the seats recovered, it is quite a boost to the whole project to be able to stand back and admire something ready to bolt back in place.

Of course, one of the most important things in any rebuild is to do the jobs in the right order. Much time is wasted by people new to the task when they either spoil a job they have finished when working on something else, or when they find they have to take a whole lot of parts off again to fit something they missed. Professional restorers save much time with cars they know well by careful planning of the work.

With an MGA, as we shall see later, it is better to get some of the repairs done to the body before it is lifted from the chassis, provided the chassis is straight and not distorting the body. If the chassis is sound and the body needs little work then don't be in a rush to part the two at all. I know it is a lot easier to work on the chassis with the body off but consider firstly just how large and heavy it is, and also just how easily it can be damaged if the sill area is weak. This is particularly relevant if all the work is carried out in a single garage where space is very limited. I have seen people just carefully raising the body a few inches to paint around the mountings, etc. before lowering it back again.

If the car is to be completely stripped and reassembled then look at the way they were built at the factory. The complete rolling chassis, engine, floor with carpets and some wiring in place had a trimmed body, with even the dashboard mounted, lowered onto the chassis. From this it can be seen that even the restorer should be able to benefit from installing the engine and getting the chassis as completely fitted up as possible before the body is lowered into place. One home restorer built some scaffolding in his garage to suspend the body above the chassis so all the trim and dashboard wiring could be completed before it was dropped down onto the chassis. Most of us will probably find it easier to install the bare body, minus even the wings and doors and fit them and trim the car at a later stage.

WORKSHOP, TOOLS AND EQUIPMENT

Although many people have carried out full restorations by the roadside, most need somewhere dry and warm to work. Unfortunately once a car is dismantled it takes up about four times as much room as it did in one piece and as the two largest components, the chassis and body, are also the most difficult to house the longer they are kept as a unit the better.

The workshop should ideally have a good strong bench with an engineer's vice, the jaws of which should be at elbow height for comfortable working. If there is room for one of those metal shelving units this is very useful to store many of the smaller components.

The number of tools needed will be governed by the amount of work to be done at home. If the restoration

of the body and the engine rebuilding is to be given to professionals then only good quality hand tools will be needed. As a minimum a set of AF sockets and spanners, together with a selection of screwdrivers, hammers and so on will be needed. For dismantling rusted components an impact wrench is very useful and some sort of angle grinder almost essential. I find one of the good quality small units taking 100 mm discs ideal. In addition to the set of AF spanners a few BA spanners - even just 2BA and 4BA - will be useful along with a set of UNF taps and dies. With the exception of some of the bolts used in aluminium castings and some of the small pan head screws used to fix small components almost all the other bolts have UNF threads.

If it is intended that specialist tasks, such as welding or spraying, are to be carried out then the equipment must be bought or hired. For home use a MIG welder is probably the safest and easiest to use but it does not have the advantage of providing a heat source for freeing rusty nuts, for example. It is also more difficult to use on thin steel. Gas equipment is expensive and for occasional use it is probably better to just let someone else do the work using their equipment. However, if a lot of restoration of bodywork is contemplated then the cost of buying a gas welding rig, and learning to use it, may be justified.

KEEPING RESTORED CARS 'ORIGINAL'

The subject of 'originality' is one bound to cause arguments. No two people can even agree on exactly what is meant by the term 'original'. To be precise a car could only be so called if it is exactly as it left the factory, same paint, tyres, batteries and so on. Obviously there are now very, very few MGAs that could possibly qualify, even if one discounted such replacements as tyres and batteries. So the term original now is taken to mean that the car looks as it did when it was built. The trouble with this definition is one of degree. Exactly how shiny were those carburettors on new cars in 1955? How smooth and polished was the paint in the engine bay and luggage compartment?

Looking now at those regular concours winning cars one can be certain that they are almost all better finished and prepared than cars that left the factory when new. M.G.s were very well built but were never expensively hand built and the finish on items like the chassis was only there to cover the bare steel. So what does that mean for the restorer? My view is that the standard one sets should be one that you are happy with. Ignore the temptation to over-restore a car if the intention is to enjoy using it. If, however, the intention is to enter and win concours then I am afraid every part must be done to the highest possible standard without over-polishing too many components as this may lead to losing rather than gaining marks. I am happiest trying to achieve a standard close to that set by Abingdon and then just enjoy the car and forget the concours. In some ways the car looks better once it has seen a little use and lost that over-bright appearance a freshly restored car can have.

One thing you do see less of now is the use of too many extra chromed fittings and polished radiators, none of which do anything for the appearance of the engine bay.

I quite like modern two-pack paint for its durability but some finishes can look a bit too shiny and 'plastic'. Some painters, however, manage to get a smooth finish that does not look much different from the original cellulose and this is fine.

The choice of paint colour is a matter of personal choice. The colour range for MGs was a bit restricted and for the later cars there wasn't any shade of green available. Although I think the cars look best in their original factory colours I can see why non-standard ones are specified. My only thoughts are that one should choose a colour that suits the car and looks in period - I really do not like some of the strong metallic shades sometimes selected.

In the end the choice of finish and standard of restoration is up to the owner but it should be borne in mind that if the car ever has to be sold the colour will have quite an effect on the price realised.

Chassis plate.

IDENTIFYING MGAs.

Chassis
The chassis number is stamped on a metal plate screwed to the bulkhead within the engine compartment. It goes without saying that as this plate is easily removed, and replacements are available, the existence of a number on a plate is no guarantee that it refers to the car it is screwed to! In addition to giving the chassis number it also gives additional information about the car. The system differs with the various models as follows:-

MGA 1500 The serial number of the car is preceded by a series of three letters and two numbers and can be decoded thus:-
First letter H refers to MGA.
Second letter D denotes two-seater.
Third letter is paint colour. A - black, D - Mineral Blue, E - Island Green, C or K - Orient Red, L - Glacier Blue, R - Old English White, T - Ash Green or Tyrolite Green.
First number 1 RHD home market, 2 RHD export market, 3 LHD, 4 North America, 5 complete knocked down kit for local assembly RHD, 6 LHD CKD kit.
Second number paint type:- 1 synthetic, 2 Synobel, 3 cellulose, 4 metallic, 5 primed, 6 cellulose body/ synthetic wings. (MGAs are almost all painted in cellulose.
The first MGA 1500 was number 10101 and the last number 68850 built in July 1959.

MGA 1600 and 1600 Mk II The chassis numbers for the later cars gave less detail than those on the 1500 and consists of the following:-
First letter G - M.G.
Second letter H - Capacity (1400 - 1999cc)
Third letter N - open two-seater, D coupe.
These three letters are followed on the 1600 Mk II by the number 2. On 1600 and 1600 Mk II the last letter in the group on left hand drive vehicles was L (for example GHN2L/100352 would be a left hand drive Mk II roadster).

Engines
Early 1500cc engine numbers were prefixed with the letters BP followed by 15 (denoting 1500cc) and GB (denoting M.G. and B for engine type). The 1500cc engine, from early 1957, had the numbering system changed to 15 (for 1500cc), GB (for M.G. and engine type), U (for centre gear change) and H (for high compression). In January 1959 the revised 15GD engine was introduced with the high starter position.

The first engine in this series was numbered 15GD-U-H/101 and was fitted to chassis 61504.

The 1600cc series of engines was type 16GA (16 for 1600cc) and the first engine was number 16GA-U-H/101 and was fitted to chassis 100352 in March 1961.

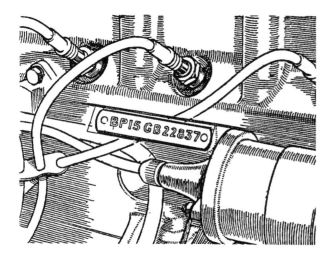

Engine number on pushrod cars.

The engine block size can be identified by the number cast into the side of them. 1500cc blocks have '1500' cast in with the earlier 15GB type still needing a blanking plate fitted over the redundant mounting for the mechanical fuel pump used on other B.M.C. models. The later 1500cc engines (GD type) did not need the plate but the number '1500' was still cast in. The 1600cc block had '1600' cast in the side but the Mk II block has '1622' instead.

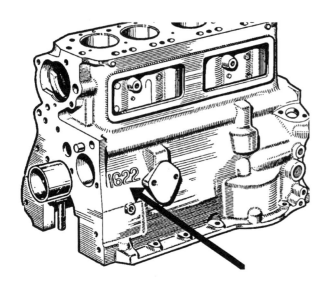

Cast number on block.

Body Number

There is a plate carrying the body number fixed to the bulkhead. This plate was attached before the body was painted and is the same colour as the rest of the body. I have not been able to produce any list of body numbers related to chassis numbers.

When looking at a car it is important to ensure that the correct power unit is fitted, or at least the correct type with the mechanical rev-counter drive. Many cars have had replacement 'B' series engines from Morris Oxford or Austin Cambridge models fitted as well as the larger, early MGB engines. If a car has a non-original engine this should be reflected in the price paid.

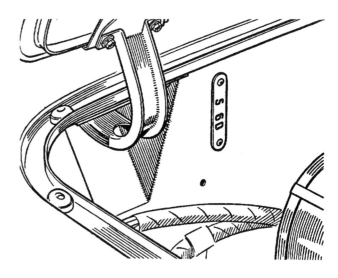

Body number.

TWIN CAM CARS

When looking at one of these, in addition to all the usual checks previously mentioned, some extra care is needed in view of the more specialised nature of the car. In particular, as it is likely to be rather more expensive, it is important to make sure that the car is exactly what it purports to be. As detailed at the end of the first chapter there were a number of body and chassis differences on the Twin Cam and if the car is being purchased dismantled then these should be checked to make sure that it is a Twin Cam you are buying and not a pushrod car with some Twin Cam engine parts.

The more usual situation is for the car to have had a replacement pushrod engine fitted after the original failed for some reason and for this engine to be either missing completely, or for it to come as separate parts.

Unless it is very cheap it is not a good idea to buy a Twin Cam without its engine. If the engine is dismantled are all the parts needed with it? These parts are now scarce and expensive and there are a number of cars around with engines built up around modified pushrod blocks but these seldom run without problems. When looking at a car with a dismantled engine ensure that the engine is re-buildable. The Twin Cam block is easily identified by the position of the engine number at the rear and by the fact that the distributor mounting point on the pushrod block is not machined on the Twin Cam. If in any doubt seek advice from an expert before making an expensive mistake.

Quite often a "spare" Twin Cam engine offered for sale will turn out to be built up from an collection of parts rejected by a previous owner when building up another engine. The engine may turn out to be virtually useless if, for example, the head has been skimmed too much, the crank cracked, the rods are from an early series engine and, perhaps, with some of the smaller auxiliary parts missing. Do not overlook the importance of ensuring that items like the water pump, thermostat housing, the carburettors and manifold and radiator header tank are all present. These items are all unique to the Twin Cam and the cost of finding replacements considerable.

There were two types of cylinder head on the Twin Cam. The later, which is preferable, had steel liners in the tappet holders but the earlier can be modified. More important is to check that the head has not been over skimmed. The factory allowance for skimming was only .020in. I am advised by the foremost specialist on these engines, Peter Wood, that the cost of modifying an early series head that has not been over skimmed to later specification would be at least £1,000, when the cost of all the parts needed are taken into consideration. I can only stress that any engine must be examined very carefully before purchase, perhaps checking the engine number against the workshop manual and parts list to see that it is made up of components appropriate to an engine built up at that stage of production. If the vendor is not happy to see you carefully examining the engine, or taking it to a specialist like Peter Wood, then don't buy it!

The spares situation with the engine is not quite as easy as the standard car, although crankshafts can be made they are expensive, and some bearings are in short supply. The cost of an engine rebuild will be at least five times that of the standard pushrod unit.

Position of Twin Cam engine number.

MGA bodies, completely trimmed and wired, are lowered onto the awaiting chassis from the upper deck.

CHAPTER THREE

CHASSIS AND RUNNING GEAR

When compared with the earlier M.G. T-types the fundamental difference between their chassis and the MGA is the change to a perimeter frame. On all the previous M.G. sports cars the occupants sat **on** the chassis whereas on the MGA they sit between the rails. Although this was necessary to lower the seats, and thus the overall height of the car, this change in design does mean that the chassis rails are more vulnerable and are certainly a lot more likely to need repairs because of rust than the previous models.

Dependent on conditions and usage most MGA chassis will have some rusting. If the car has spent most of it's life in a warm, dry climate then this will probably be fairly limited and easily repaired, but a car that has been regularly used in wet conditions, often on salted roads, could well need a considerable amount of work.

Whatever the condition of the chassis the first task is to check the dimensions to see if there is any distortion as a result of accident damage. There is a detailed dimensional drawing in the workshop manual and this gives all the data needed to check the important measurements. The advice given is to carry out a drop test onto a suitably flat surface. Unfortunately the home garage floor is the best most of us have so this will have to do. Before starting it is ESSENTIAL that the floor is checked for flatness with long straight boards and a level first. If all the dimensions given are to be checked then it is no good if the floor slopes, or has

bulges or dips in the centre. If the floor is uneven and there is reason to suppose that the chassis will need very careful checking then try to find somewhere else to measure it or use some heavy grade chipboard panels, or similar, to create a flat surface.

The chassis check can be carried out with the car assembled, although it is obviously easier if the body is off the chassis. If the car is checked assembled this is when the completely flat surface is essential because the datum points on the chassis (the body mounting holes and front suspension mounts) need to be transferred to the flat surface using a plumb line. When doing this it is worth paying the small amount needed to buy a proper plumb bob, or turn one up on a lathe.

When checking the measurements on a complete car make sure that it is on jacks set exactly level. The straight side section of the chassis frame should be parallel to the floor and packing pieces used on the axle stands until this is achieved. Considerable time and care must be taken when transferring the marks to the flat surface and in carrying out the measurements - sloppy work is a complete waste of time and may lead to carrying out unnecessary repairs.

Most people carrying out major chassis repairs will have removed the body and it is considerably easier to measure the chassis when stripped. If a flat surface is not available, set up the chassis on stands, packed level with small wedges of wood, and check with a good spirit level. Then use a long, straight piece of wood resting on blocks, and also set up level, onto which the datum points should be transferred. This can be moved around to take the various measurements. Although it will not be possible to check the centre line so accurately the results will be good enough to assess the extent of any distortion.

The most common reasons for damage are as a result of either front or rear collisions. A knock on the front corner, or a front wheel, will usually force the chassis upwards, kinking the bracing bar running from behind the front suspension to the scuttle. To correct this the leg of the chassis has to be forced back into position with jacks after the bracing bar has been cut through (it is later welded together again). Often it is easy to spot any distortion in this area as the bracing bar will ripple and this can be felt when examining a car. If the front wheel has been forced inwards against the chassis then this will often cause it to bend.

A rear end accident will force the chassis to bow outwards above the rear axle and to buckle around the rear of the centre section - usually in front of the cross tube behind the seats. If distortion is considerable then consider using a chassis specialist to pull it straight on one of his jigs.

It is worth remembering that the mounting plates on top of the front suspension cross member should be flat and in line with each other. A straight edge laid across the both of them will soon check this. Remember, the most important start to any good restoration is a sound chassis that conforms to the original maker's dimensions. This must be right before any other work is done as it is little use having a nice shiny paint finish if the car does not steer well or if the body is being distorted by a bent chassis.

As I said earlier, rust is a big problem with the MGA chassis. Virtually no corrosion protection was applied from new and the design effectively ensures that it will rust badly in a wet climate. Mind you I am not blaming the designers of the time as they did not envisage us still wanting to use the cars so many years after they were originally built. They had hoped we would be buying new M.G.s every few years!

Now let us look at the main problem areas and how they can be repaired. The floorboards on the MGA are made of wood and this holds moisture, particularly around the edges where the boards sit on the supports welded to the inner edge of the chassis. This moisture rusts the side of the chassis frame, eventually allowing water to run right through into the box section. Water inside the box will soon rust out the bottom of it reducing its strength considerably. Of course, the angle-iron brackets that hold the floorboards will themselves also be badly damaged by this damp.

In addition to water creeping in around the floorboards it also manages to rust the outside of the frame where mud and debris are trapped between the frame and the body, and also where water runs down by the front door pillar. In this area there was a felt pad placed within the chassis to stop noise travelling along the frame from the engine bay. This pad soaks up the water and creates an excellent environment for rust. The rear spring hanger area is also prone to rusting and should be checked.

REPAIRING RUSTED CHASSIS

The first step is to find out just how much rust there is and, in my view, the best way to do this is to take the chassis to a good shot blast specialist and have it cleaned. Before taking it to them you should remove as much grease, oil and undersealing as you can as this clogs the blasting material and the operator will not be very happy. If the blasting is carried out well it will reveal all the areas of rust damage, but not necessarily any rusting from the inside out.

As soon as the chassis is blasted a protecting coat of etch primer should be applied to stop any further rusting whilst repairs are carried out.

The chassis on an MGA is constructed of 16 gauge steel and any repairs must be made of the same material. Parts to replace the straight centre sections are available from suppliers as are the floorboard support brackets and the battery carriers. All welding on the chassis is best done with electric welding equipment to minimise heat distortion. Any cutting will need to be done with a hacksaw, plasma cutter or angle grinder as it is rather too thick for tin snips. However carefully repairs are carried out to the side rail it is all too easy to distort the chassis unless it is adequately braced. The easiest way to do this is to bolt lengths of angle iron between the top of the bulkhead stiffener and the shock absorber mounting points at the rear. This brace will stop the chassis folding up in the centre as repairs are carried out. Careful measurements must be taken before any metal is removed and perhaps templates made from timber to enable the width, etc. to be checked as work proceeds.

The side members are in two pieces and if damage is confined to the inner section this should be cut out and replaced with a new rail, leaving the outer rail in place. Once a section is removed the extent of the rusting from the inside out can be assessed. Through this hole it is possible to sand blast the inside of the box section to reveal the full extent of rusting if the necessary equipment is available. Work should be carried out on only one side of the car at a time and the dimensions checked at frequent intervals.

A word here about welding. The chassis is vital to the strength of the car and all welding must be to a good standard. The home MIG welding equipment is capable of producing welds of sufficient strength, provided it is used correctly, but if there is any doubt then the work should be entrusted to a specialist. When inserting repair sections these should first be tacked in place at intervals and then seam welded all round. Once the edges have been ground off flat, the repair can be undetectable.

The floorboard support brackets can be bought with all the captive nuts fixed in place although the small clips that hold the petrol and brake pipes on the offside of the chassis are not usually there and will need to be attached. After checking from the old rails the height these need

to be fixed to the chassis side members it is a simple matter to weld the new ones in place. Where the damage is confined to a small area then this can be cut out, or ground back to sound metal, and a patch welded in. 'G' cramps are useful to hold the metal in place.

The battery carriers are usually badly corroded and they are available as replacements parts, or can be made up from angle-iron. Before cutting off the remains of the old carriers carefully note their position so that the replacements are fixed in the same places. If all the repairs have been carefully done the resulting chassis should be as strong as the original and will not have been distorted by the repair process - now we can look at how to keep it in good condition.

Once the chassis is ready to receive the final finish the material to be used can be considered. However, as mentioned earlier, the final finish should not be applied if the chassis is to be used as a jig on which to build up the body. Inevitably this will result in damage and much frustration will result if the whole job needs doing again. Better to leave this until the messy work on the body is finished.

Originally the chassis received only a coat of black chassis paint when built and this was fairly roughly applied. These days, however, many people prefer a much more elaborate, and better looking, appearance and there are a number of finishes that are suitable.

For home application a coat of etch primer followed by

A repair section for the chassis rails. These are available for both inner and outer parts of both the left and right hand rails. The piece illustrated has the cut out for the square section cross member and is folded where appropriate.

primer and gloss black top coat in cellulose or chassis enamel can be used. A good finish is obtained if the surface is first filled and rubbed down to remove any imperfections. Although attractive, this finish is not all that durable or resistant to stone chipping.

Modern two-pack paints are a little more durable but need the use of air-fed masks and a proper spray booth to apply them. Again the finish can be very attractive. Another alternative is to have the whole chassis stove enamelled or powder coated; the latter is now very popular. However, both of these finishes are only as good as the preparation the firm doing the work carries out. Any slight surface rusting allowed on the chassis before the final coats are applied will eventually cause problems.

A point to remember is that the cars will now probably receive much kinder use than they had in their first thirty-odd years. Mileages are now low and the cars are seldom used all year round. For this reason any well protected chassis is likely to last for as long as you want to keep the car. After painting, 'Waxoyl' or some similar preparation should be injected into the box members to guard against any further rusting from the inside out. After finishing the captive nuts should be cleaned out with a tap to ease assembly at later stages.

The front extension on later cars differs from that on the early 1500s. If a roll bar is to be fitted to one of these earlier cars then it is easier to fit one of these later extensions which have the modifications for the roll bar incorporated.

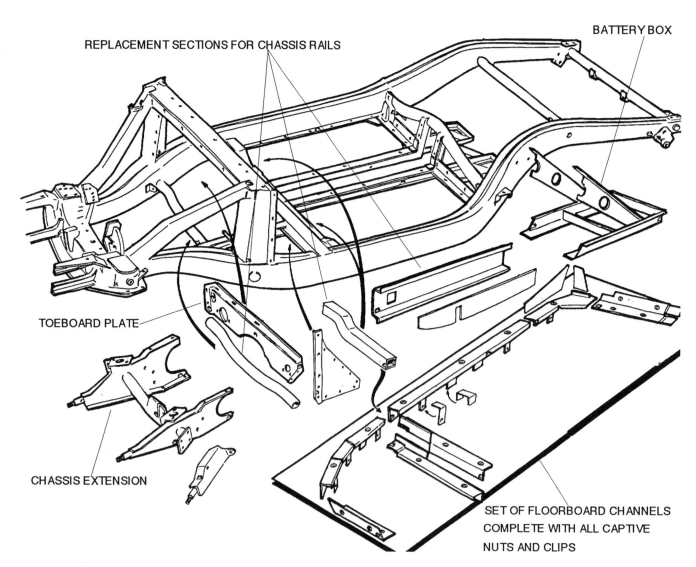

REPLACEMENT SECTIONS FOR CHASSIS RAILS

BATTERY BOX

TOEBOARD PLATE

CHASSIS EXTENSION

SET OF FLOORBOARD CHANNELS COMPLETE WITH ALL CAPTIVE NUTS AND CLIPS

An illustration from a suppliers parts book showing the chassis repair sections available. (Courtesy Anglo Parts)

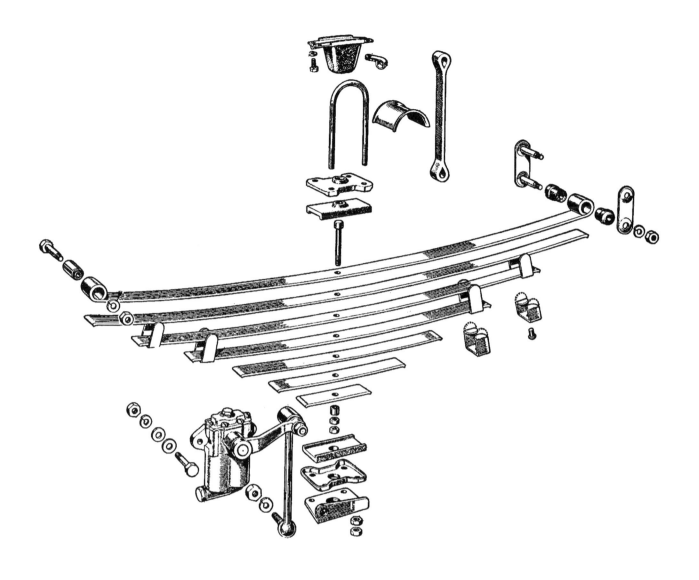

SUSPENSION

Springs

New springs are available and, in addition to the standard units, there are uprated springs for competition use. However, I would not recommend changing the standard specification without carefully considering the effect of such a change and perhaps discussing this with a specialist. Examination of the car before it is dismantled will give some idea of the state of the old units and the ride height and general stance of the car will show if any of them have sagged. If the old springs look sound consider just having them cleaned and repainted rather than replaced. All the rubber bushes and the metalastic bush at the front of the rear springs should be replaced as a matter of course.

The front springs on the early 1500 (up to chassis 15151) were 409 lbs/in. rate and these were changed to stiffer springs of 480 lbs/in. from chassis 15152 but the ride height was unchanged. These later springs can be fitted to the earlier cars. The Twin Cam front springs were of the same rate but were slightly longer (9.09in. as against 8.68in. to counteract the greater weight). If shorter springs are fitted to lower the suspension remember that the ride height is lowered by approximately twice the amount the spring is shortened because it is mounted about half way along the wishbone arms.

Shock absorbers

The front shock absorbers in particular must be in good condition and work well if the car is to handle correctly. As they act both as dampers and as the top mounting point for the front swivel pin link they take quite a beating in hard use. As most are now over thirty years old they are often well past their best. Unfortunately some of the reconditioned units available from time to time are of little use. Often these have had no more than a set of seals and a coat of paint and have never been properly set up, to match the specified bump and rebound rates, by the restorer. However, some good restorers do exist and although their services are not cheap they do get good results. I would recommend having your units restored by a good specialist or, as an alternative, fitting the MGB-based new units now available. These are, however, slightly taller than the originals and the inner wing may need to be cut back a bit to accommodate them. At the time of writing some new units are being developed that are direct replacements for the originals without any modification being needed to the body.

Check that the arms of the front dampers are not bent. They are not all that strong and a heavy bang on a front wheel can distort them, which will upset the steering geometry.

The rear dampers also need to be looked at carefully and because they are hidden away they are usually neglected and allowed to run dry. Fortunately new units are available if the old ones are beyond repair.

As with the springs, uprated units are available but I would not recommend fitting these unless competition work is contemplated and then only if the whole set up of the car is considered. There are a number of conversions to telescopic dampers available but I do not have any experience of these and anyway would prefer to stay with the factory set-up for road use. A standard MGA rides and handles well enough for most people and with the deterioration in road surfaces seen in recent years stiffening up the suspension would not seem a particularly good idea.

FRONT SUSPENSION SWIVEL PIN ASSEMBLY

The front suspension is of a design first developed in the late 1930s. This was brought into use after the war and the first M.G. to be fitted with it was the Y-type and this chassis was modified to become the TD and TF.

The MGA suspension, although similar to that fitted to earlier cars and later to the MGB, is unique in almost every detail and few parts are interchangeable.

The swivel pin is not perhaps the strongest item on the car and should be inspected carefully if it to be re-used. If the car has had an accident or a bang on a front wheel then it is quite likely to be bent. Remember too that modern tyres are much better than their 1950s counterparts and their grip is much more than the original equipment crossplies. These modern tyres impart far higher loads on the suspension and in particular the swivel pin.

The screw threads on the pin and in the trunnions wear and it may be advisable to replace these as a set if the threads on either one are much worn. The new thread on a pin will very soon knock any 'high spots' off the corresponding part worn thread in the trunnion and movement between the two components will result. Before assembling the new components to the car check that they are free. Quite a number of these new parts are made with too tight a tolerance on the threads and if assembled as they are will result in very stiff steering and a lack of self-centering with a consequent lack of stability at speed. In the worst cases use a fine grinding paste on the threads and wind the trunnion up and down a few times to free it off - cleaning ALL the paste off before assembly.

Again, before assembling the front suspension examine the wishbone arms for damage and the suspension pan for cracks. If a roll-bar is to be fitted, arms with the necessary reinforcing and mounting holes could be used. Later cars (from chassis 66574) had spring pans with roll-bar mounting holes on them. All these suspension components benefit from being powder coated after shot blasting - it saves many hours cleaning them up.

I suggest that the front suspension be trial assembled without the spring in place to check all the fits before final assembly. Many MGAs are assembled by people who do not appreciate the exact function of all the parts and without reading the workshop manual carefully enough. In particular it is vital that the distance tube is long enough to allow sufficient end float (.008 to .013in.) of the king pin swivel links. If this end float is not present the suspension could be SOLID, i.e. the only springing will be in the tyres and rather peculiar handing will result. Look carefully at the order of

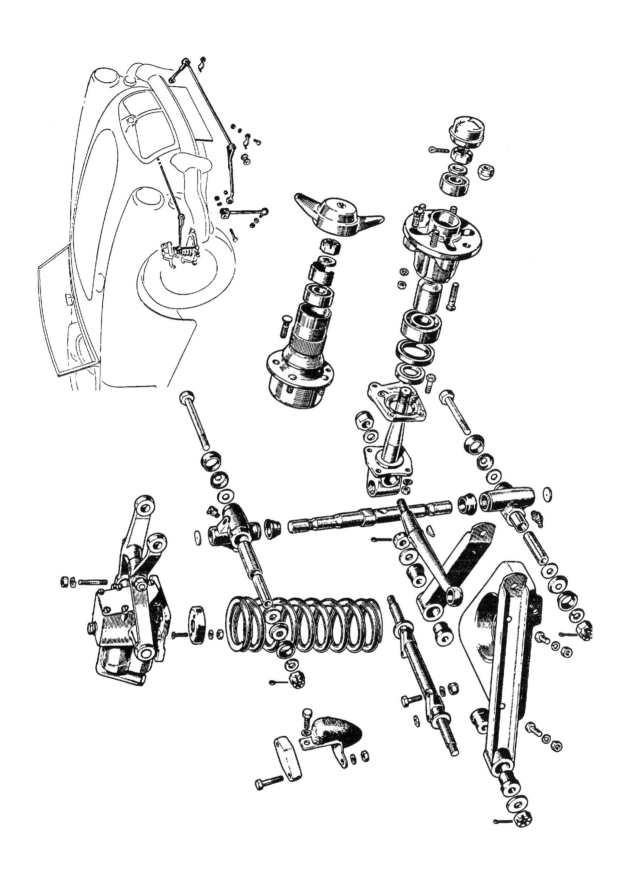

assembly of the thrust washer, seal and seal support as these are often wrongly assembled. After trial assembly without the spring the suspension should move up and down freely and the stub axle should move freely, under its own weight, from side to side.

New rubbers must be fitted on the inner wishbone arms and these should protrude equally from each side of the arm. The nut should be tightened up with the arm parallel to the ground to minimise the distortion of the bushes in use. Note the instruction in the workshop manual to leave final tightening of the spring pan bolts on final assembly until the weight is on the wheel, and also remember to grease the ends of the coil springs to ensure they can move as the suspension works.

The wheel bearings and seals should be examined. Replace the seals as a matter of course and clean out all the old grease from the bearings and then look for any sign of wear, pitting or a 'gritty' feel when revolved. If in doubt replace. Before refitting press the bearings into a suitable grease until it is forced right through and clean off the surplus. The bearings are fitted to the hub with the distance tube placed with the taper towards the smaller, outer bearing. When assembled as described in the workshop manual and the hub nut tightened, the hub should spin freely on the axle.

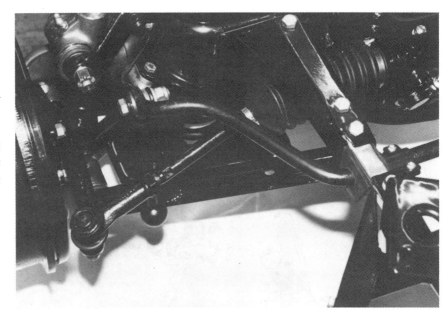

The front suspension on the 1500. The mounting for the anti-roll bar can be seen. The front chassis extension is the later type with provision for the bar mountings.

Another view of the anti-roll bar mounting on the MGA. Once the car has run a few miles the tightness of all bolts must be checked.

The shock absorber mounting bolts must be well tightened and checked again when the car has been used for a while.

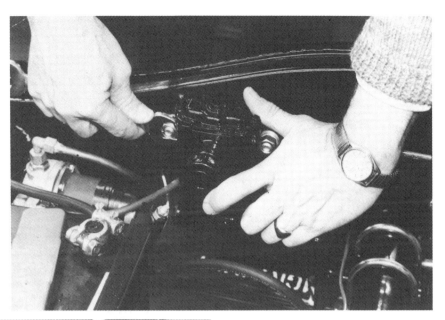

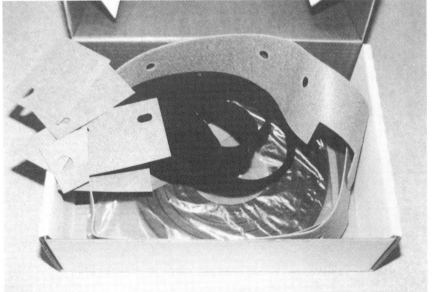

Kits containing all the cork, felt and rubber pieces needed to mount the body on the chassis are available.

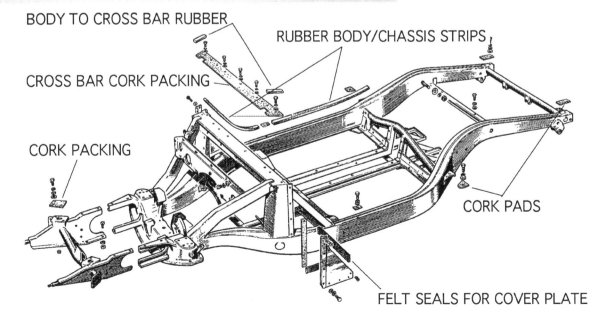

BODY TO CROSS BAR RUBBER

RUBBER BODY/CHASSIS STRIPS

CROSS BAR CORK PACKING

CORK PACKING

CORK PADS

FELT SEALS FOR COVER PLATE

Cork pad in place on chassis before body is mounted. It is easier if these packing pieces are lightly fixed with some adhesive, or a dab of mastic sealer, to stop them moving as the body is lowered into place.

Here the front toeboard has a cut out for the higher mounted starter found on the later 1500 and all 1600 models. I find it easier to paint the floorboards and toeboards before they are installed and to seal them to the chassis rails with mastic strips. A useful form of this mastic is sold as gutter sealant and comes in rolls about 15mm wide.

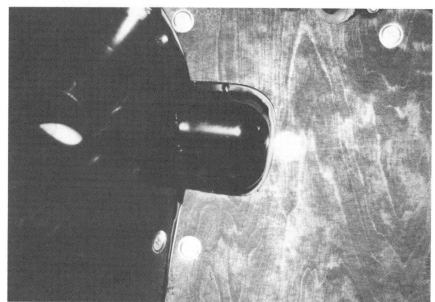

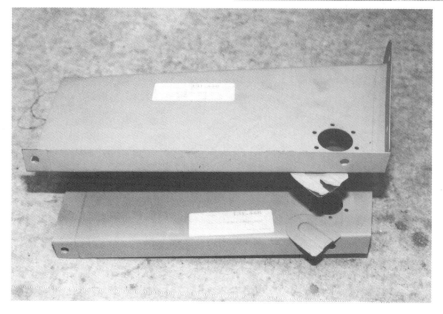

The propshaft covers are often rusty and battered but new ones are available. The one shown here has provision for fixing the seat belt mounting points. The drain channels can also be seen.

STEERING

The rack and pinion steering on MGAs is a reliable mechanism that gives very little trouble in service provided it is kept lubricated. Usually replacements are limited to the track rod ends and the rubber gaiters. However, if wear does occur in the rack this is normally confined to the centre portion and cannot be adjusted out by removing shims as it makes the rack over-tight on full lock. Fortunately new racks and pinions are available, as are re-manufactured units to convert cars from left to right hand drive. That is the good news, but the bad is that some of these, at the time of writing, are not as well made as the original items and are causing some problems in use. The only advice I can give here is to buy from a reputable source and to go back to them if you strike problems.

Stripping the rack in the home workshop is complicated by the requirement for two special tools to dismantle the tie rod ball joint housing. As any sort of 'heavy hammer' method of undoing this housing is only likely to result in damaging it, try to borrow or make the correct tools as illustrated in the manual or leave the job to professionals.

The steering rack should not be too stiff. Reject any rebuilt, or new, unit that is very tight. When mounted on the chassis, without the steering column fitted, it should be possible to push and pull the rack from side to side just with the grip provided by holding on to the track rod end. Something that is overlooked, especially when converting from left to right hand drive, is steering rack alignment. The workshop manual gives details of the alignment procedure and position of shims, and this is very important as the steering could be stiff if the rack is misaligned.

The steering column universal joint usually does not give trouble but if it is worn both replacement and rebuilt units are available, as well as parts to recondition your own unit.

There are two types of steering column fitted to MGAs. One, which was an optional extra, allowed for the steering wheel to be adjusted in and out. Both the inner column and outer tube are different on these columns. The felt bushes in the column should be replaced if the old ones are worn. I have seen two types over the years, one is impregnated with graphite grease and the other is just plain felt. If fitting the latter soak in light oil for a time before fitting.

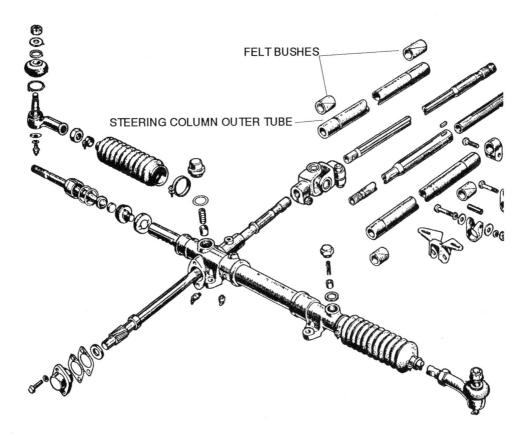

FELT BUSHES

STEERING COLUMN OUTER TUBE

LHD - RHD CONVERSIONS

With many cars being repatriated from export markets in recent years quite a number of candidates for conversion from left to right hand drive exist. Forgetting the ethics of changing the car's original specification there are many reasons why such a conversion may be a good idea - not the least of which may be safety.

Luckily the MGA is relatively easy to convert as the car was designed from the outset to be built for either market. The list of parts required is short and are now available from most suppliers.

The pedal box and blanking plate merely swap sides but the clutch pedal needs changing, as does the throttle pedal. Of course, the dashboard needs to be changed and this involves quite a lot of work on the wiring and cable runs. The new dashboard will need painting in body colour unless it is to go on a Twin Cam or 1600 Mk II where it is covered in rexine to match the upholstery.

Electrical fittings, such as the dip-switch and headlamps, have to be considered but on the 1500 the dip-switch can be changed over without modification, whereas on the later cars a new bracket is needed.

Carpets will need changing as only the driver's side had a heel mat.

LIST OF PARTS REQUIRED

Steering rack RHD. Either a complete new or rebuilt unit. Often these are supplied as exchange units for the old LHD rack.

Clutch pedal. This is a different shape to the LHD version. Some suppliers will modify the old pedal.

Throttle pedal with bush, bracket, bolt, distance tube, pedal stop and stop bracket.

Dashboard.

Brake and clutch pipes to suit changed master cylinder position.

Rev-counter and speedometer cables.

Dip-switch bracket (1600/1600 Mk II only).

Headlamp units for LH dipping.

Tonneau cover.

Wiper arms (also park position on motor modified)

The dual master cylinder and the pedal box will transfer from the left to right hand side of the car. The blanking plate then needs moving to the left hand side. It is a good idea to replace any worn clevis pins in the brake and clutch linkage.

The pedals on the right and left hand drive cars. This is a left hand drive 1500 with the steering column removed.

The end of the cross shaft that transfers the movement of the throttle pedal to the right hand side of the car.

The same car after conversion to right hand drive with new pedals fitted.

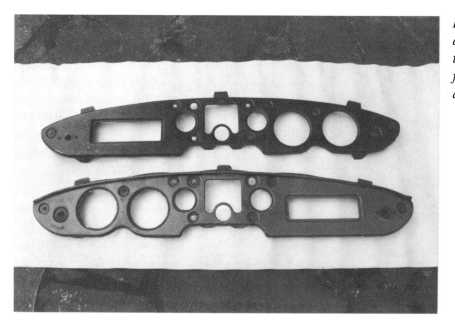

Replacement RHD dashboards are available for the roadster but not for the coupe. Below is the arrangement for the clutch master and slave cylinders on the RHD cars.

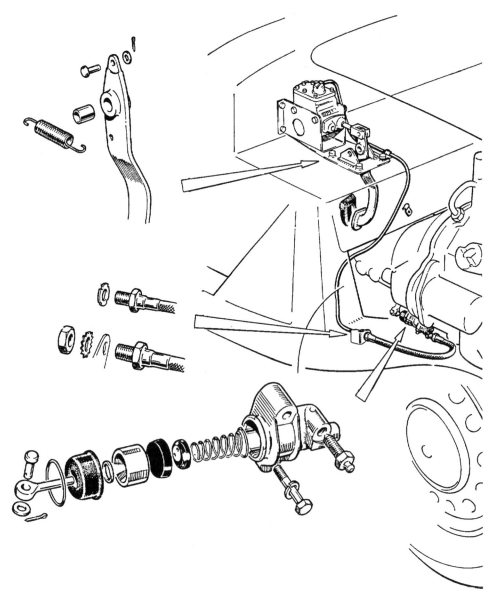

CHAPTER FOUR

BODYWORK

When the MGA was conceived in the early 1950s corrosion protection was not high on the list of priorities for the designers. In this they were not alone and I cannot think of any car designed at that time, certainly in this country, where much thought was given to making it last beyond four or five years. The consequence of this is a body designed with a number of rust traps that ensure that almost every MGA that has seen much use in a damp climate will have serious rusting, no matter how careful the owner has been.

I hope these remarks will not be taken as a criticism of the superb team that designed and built such a beautiful car with what, in current terms, would be a laughably small budget. However, as restorers we have to live with the consequences of the shortcomings of the design when trying to return the cars to perfect condition.

The MGA body is probably one of the most difficult to work on of any M.G. two seater. The standard of care over fits of panels must be of a high order if the car is to look as good as the day it first left the factory. I am sure that you have all seen cars where the doors do not fit, the wings do not line up and the wing piping, a very tricky area, does not fit. The only way to achieve perfection is to make sure that any new parts fitted conform to the original dimensions and that the work is checked at all stages for fits. Having a door pillar even a small amount out of line will spoil the alignment of the rest of the panels on that side of the car.

There are replacement parts available for almost all the panels of the MGA body. Indeed, Moss Europe at Darlington will even supply you with a completely new body utilising only the doors, boot and bonnet from the old body and even these can be supplied new if required. However, that said do not expect any of the replacement panels, or indeed the new body, to be EXACT copies of the originals. Unlike wings for the MGB or Midget, for example, all the parts for the MGA have to be made by hand. All of the original press tools have long since been destroyed and the parts now made will have been hand formed using a wheeling machine and conventional panel beating skills. Nevertheless, those parts that are available are a lot better than nothing at all and it is up to the restorer to make the best use of what is to hand. Anglo Parts in Belgium will supply a rebuilt exchange body at a fixed price whatever the condition of the old body. At the time of writing the same company are developing rear wings for the MGA which are pressed rather than formed by hand and these should be easier to fit.

TOOLS

The amount of equipment needed depends largely on what work is to be done at home and how much left to the specialists. Also, of course, on just how bad the bodywork is; lucky is the man with a car from a dry climate that needs only minor repairs! The body is made of much thinner steel - 20 gauge - than the chassis and consequently is rather less easy to weld with home MIG equipment. The difficulty is finding a setting low enough to reduce the chance of burning holes in the metal but one that will still provide a continuous arc. Many of the cheaper machines seem to provide a poor output on the lower settings. The ideal for welding thin steel is gas, but equipment is expensive and the techniques to use it well take a long time to acquire. In practise a good MIG will do most jobs so long as edge to edge welds are avoided where possible.

This brings me on to another useful tool for use with the welder - a joggling tool. These form a lip on the edge of the piece of steel allowing for overlapping joints. These can then be easily welded by drilling small holes in the upper piece and welding through the holes to unite them. To hold the steel in place for welding self-locking clamps with jaws of various sizes are available. These can be found, singly or in sets, at tool shops and autojumbles, and unless a large amount of work is contemplated the cheaper variety will suffice.

To cut steel, good quality shears, angle grinder and pad saw will do most jobs. The thin body steel can be cut easily with shears although some of the mechanical 'nibblers' now available to attach to an electric drill are useful for cutting large areas without distortion.

A certain amount of panel beating to make parts fit, or shape sheet steel for repairs, will be needed and a good quality universal dolly and a couple of hammers will cover most needs. Remember, to stretch metal use a hammer with a rounded face and to shrink it use one with the cross-hatching especially produced for the purpose. A square edged, flat billet of steel, or the tail of a large vice, is useful for folding steel to make small brackets, etc.

Final sanding of areas of filler is much easier with a random orbit sander and some small examples are now available with self-adhesive abrasive pads in various grades. These smaller units quite often have dust collection bags as well.

BEFORE WORK STARTS

The order of work will depend largely on how badly rusted the body is. If there is comparatively little rust, and the chassis is likewise little damaged, it may be better to consider leaving the body on the car and restoring it as a unit. The advantage is that there is less

chance of doing any further damage to the body and all the fits of doors, etc. will be unchanged. This is also the only sensible solution where space is very limited. However, access to the chassis is very much easier if the body is out of the way and lifting the engine and gearbox out is a much less nerve wracking experience.

Unless the centre section of the body has entirely disappeared, and there is little to work from, the amateur restorer may find it better to restore the body as far as possible before removing it to start work on the chassis. Provided the check of the chassis has revealed no major distortion to be remedied that could affect the fit of the body, making good any rusted part of the body before removing it from the chassis will ensure that it does not bend in the middle, distorting the door gaps. Being cautious by nature I would always brace the body across the top of the cockpit before removing it from the chassis, even if it looks sound. The best way to do this is to bolt a strong brace between the front and rear of the cockpit. A piece of square section steel tube with flat plates welded on both ends and drilled to enable them to be bolted to the fixing holes for the cockpit edge trim is ideal.

Before any metal is cut away, and certainly before the body is removed from the chassis, detailed measurements must be taken to ensure that the new parts can be fitted in exactly the right position. It is well worth while making up patterns and templates to use when fitting the new parts. The critical measurements are the width of the door opening, width of body across the car and the placing of the body mounting brackets. It is all to easy to throw the fit of the panels on the whole of one side of the car out of line with one quite small error in measuring.

CLEANING UP THE BODY

A lot of sheer hard work is needed at this stage to ascertain exactly how much metalwork needs repair. The paint will have to be removed to reveal any previous 'bodged' repairs and hidden rust. It is possible to use sand or bead blasting for some areas but NEVER on the wings, bonnet, boot lid, doors or any flat areas like the scuttle, shroud or duct panel. I have seen perfectly sound parts totally ruined by over-enthusiastic use of the blasting equipment and once a panel has been stretched and rippled there is no way of restoring it satisfactorily.

I would use chemical strippers on the paintwork and leave the sand blasting for those hidden areas of inner wings and inner sills. Although tedious at least rubbing down by hand will not damage the metal further. Once all the paint and rust has been removed apply a protective coating of etch primer to prevent any further rusting. One word of caution, the aluminium doors, bonnet and boot are easily damaged so do not be too enthusiastic with the scrapers and sanders!

STARTING WORK ON REPAIRS

By this time it should be evident exactly how much metal will need replacing. As I have said previously, the replacement panels are good but nowhere near as good as sound original parts. The wings, for example, are not exactly the right shape and require quite a lot of time and skill to fit properly. For this reason, if not for cost saving, try to retain the originals as far as possible. Repair sections to replace the lower parts of wings, the front of the shroud and the lower part of the rear deck, are available. Very careful measuring is needed before cutting away the rusted sections. To join the new to the old the easiest method for the home restorer with only MIG equipment is to use a joggling tool to overlap the panels. These can then by joined by plug welding through holes drilled in the top piece of metal. The seam line can then be filled with lead before painting. The technique of 'lead loading' is not difficult to acquire and kits containing the necessary materials are readily available. I would much prefer to use lead to fill where possible as it make a lot more permanent and watertight join than the usual 'two part' fillers.

One area on an MGA body where rusting occurs and which is difficult to repair easily is the section around the wing bolts. The wings are bolted to the front and rear body sections and inner wings and this area is a moisture trap. In the worst cases the rust takes hold in both the edge of the top panel and in the top of the inner wings and both may need sections replaced. As you can appreciate, without some sort of template to work to, it is all too easy to make a mistake when replacing metal and end up with nothing fitting properly. Provided enough of the original metal remains then make up a pattern from strong card or thin aluminium to give both the position of the bolt holes and the shape of the inner edge of the wing. Use this pattern to check as work proceeds. There are no replacement sections available although complete panels are produced. However, these are both expensive and require some work to fit

correctly. Usually damage is confined to just part of the join, often the front, and small pieces can be shaped by hand and welded in to replace the rusted sections.

The door openings are critical and great care must be taken to align the door pillars correctly. With the bottom edge of the chassis as the datum line, the sill should be parallel and the pillars absolutely vertical. The front door pillar is square to the axis of the car but the rear is angled 4 degrees to the rear to allow the door to open. The inner faces of the sills are parallel to one another and to the side members of the chassis. After lightly fixing the 'F' section of the door pillars and sill in place, hang the door and check the fit. Also try the wings to check their fit against the door.

When replacing panels that were originally spot welded together then it is necessary to remove these spot welds as neatly as possible. The easiest way to do this is to centre punch the spot weld, preferably from the side of the join where the panel is to be discarded, and to drill the weld out either with a high speed drill bit or with one of those fancy circular saw cutters especially made for the job. A blow from the sharpened edge of a strong blade between the two pieces of metal will also help. Plug welding with a MIG will simulate the original spot welds when the panel is replaced. Current MOT regulations will mean that a car can fail if any of the body panels are brazed rather than welded even though the body is not structural on an MGA. For this reason it is better to weld all repairs to avoid problems later on.

As it is usually nearest to the accident, the front of MGA bodies seem often to have suffered damage. When repairing this area the radiator grill must be offered up frequently to check for fit - it is very annoying to find out once the car is painted that the piping keeps on falling out because the radiator grill does not touch the body all the way round. Incidentally replacement grills are not such a good fit as the original so make sure that the grill used to check the fit is the one that will be used on the car.

When the front duct panel and the shroud have been badly distorted, carefully drilling out the spot welds that attach the duct panel to the inner wings and removing the panel completely is the best solution. There are new panels available that are very accurately cut and bolting one of these in place on the chassis will give a good idea where the inner wings and front of the shroud need (continues on page 62)

A basic tool for any restorer is a MIG welder. The model seen here is one of the middle priced units with a cooling fan and a reasonable range of settings. For small jobs the standard sized roll of wire fitted is sufficient but a larger one can be used. The adjustable valve, not usually fitted as standard, seen in the lower picture gives a visible indication of the gas flow to the shield.

Correct alignment of the door pillars and the inner sill are vital. Professional restorers construct elaborate jigs - such as the one seen in the top picture - to ensure good alignment and panel fits. The complete body sides can be purchased (centre picture) if all the dimensions of the original body have been lost, but these are expensive. Below new body sides are aligned on the jig as the rest of the panels are fitted.

PLAN VIEW OF INNER SILL

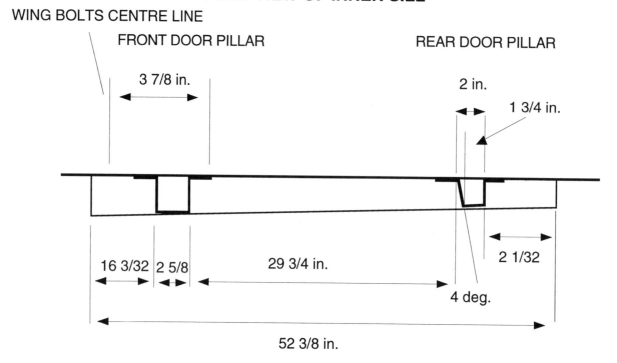

WING BOLTS CENTRE LINE

FRONT DOOR PILLAR

REAR DOOR PILLAR

3 7/8 in.

2 in.

1 3/4 in.

16 3/32   2 5/8

29 3/4 in.

2 1/32

4 deg.

52 3/8 in.

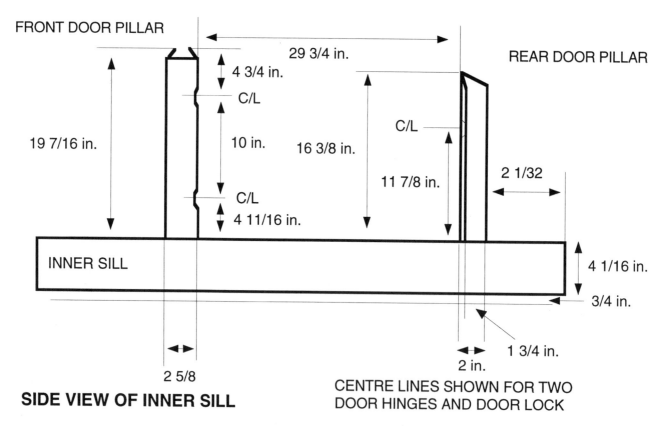

FRONT DOOR PILLAR

29 3/4 in.

REAR DOOR PILLAR

4 3/4 in.

C/L

19 7/16 in.

10 in.

16 3/8 in.

C/L

C/L

2 1/32

11 7/8 in.

4 11/16 in.

INNER SILL

4 1/16 in.

3/4 in.

2 5/8

1 3/4 in.

2 in.

SIDE VIEW OF INNER SILL

CENTRE LINES SHOWN FOR TWO
DOOR HINGES AND DOOR LOCK

This dimensional drawing was prepared by John Underwood to illustrate his excellent lectures on the MGA body at M.G. Car Club MGA Rebuild Seminars. He stresses that the dimensions are APPROXIMATE and should not be taken as gospel and are for use only when there not enough of the original body left to take measurements from. In all cases offer up the door and wings to check fits before finally welding all the parts in place.

The front body mounting and the body to chassis closing plate are seen in the top picture. Replacement inner wing sections are spot, or plug, welded to the new sides (centre). The boot floor is often rusted and here part of a new floor has been used to replace the affected section (lower picture).

The duct panel is often badly creased as seen here (top) and replacement panels produced to very fine tolerances are available (centre). Removing all the spot welds and replacing the entire panel helps alignment. In the lower picture a new duct panel and new front sections of the shroud are welded together.

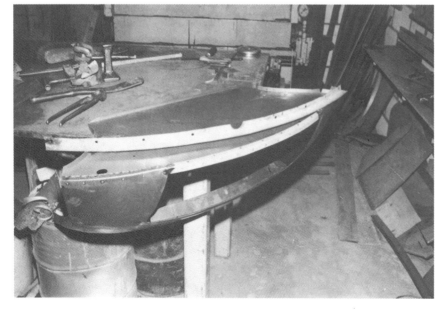

The new front section is united with the rest of the body (above). Part of the sides of the shroud needed replacing and care was taken to check the fit of the bonnet and wings. The lower part of the rear deck suffers both from rust and accident damage and if it is replaced check fit of both the boot lid and wings as work proceeds. (left and below).

The soft aluminium on the boot lid is often damaged and new skins are available. If the metal frame is badly rusted complete new boot lids are available (top picture). When fitting the sill always have the door in place to check clearances - especially that there is sufficient room for the door seal (right). Repair sections to replace damaged sections of the wings are available but before finally welding check the fit of the wing (below).

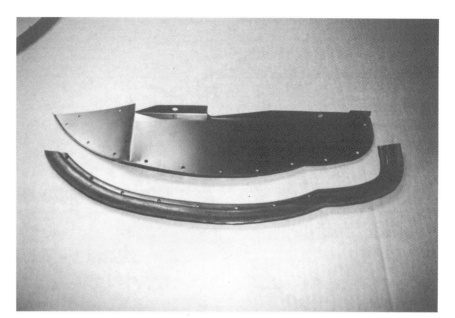

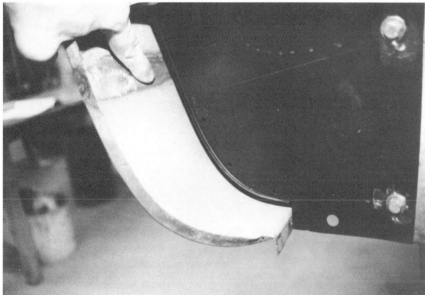

Accurately made splash plates and rubber seals are available and these can be used to check the shape when repairing wings (top and left). Below is a new rear wing produced on press tools that is a better fit than the hand formed items usually sold.

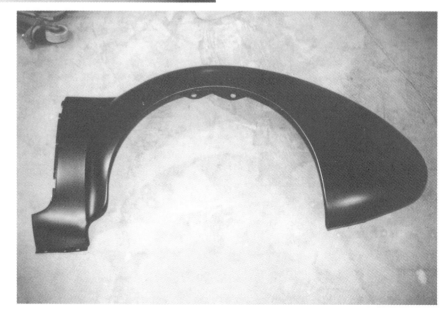

A rear wing is offered up but does not fit the sill properly and drastic surgery is needed. The lower end is cut off and a piece is inserted to bridge the gap. Although this may seem a lot of work, it is vital that all the fits on the body are right or it will never look as it should.

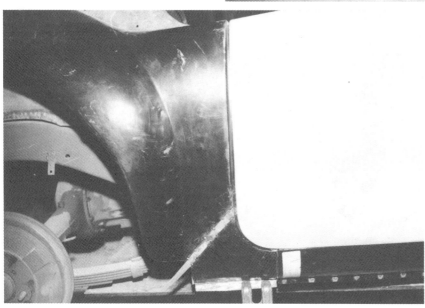

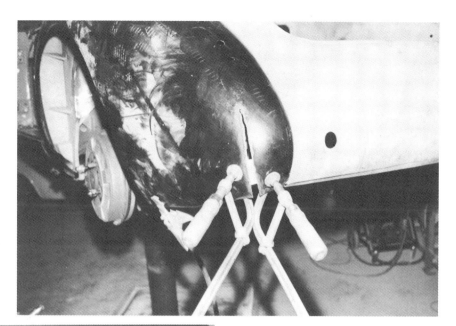

The back of the wing also needed a split to align it properly (above). When fitting new or repaired wings check that all the correct mounting holes and captive nuts are there. The pictures (left and below) are of original front wings. A packing strip fits between the vertical line of captive nuts at the back of the front wing and the body side to align the wing to the door and this can be adjusted to suit to allow the door to be mounted far enough out for the door seal to fit.

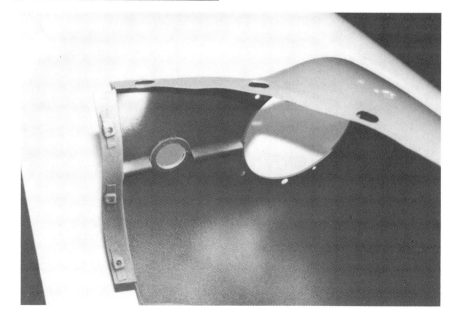

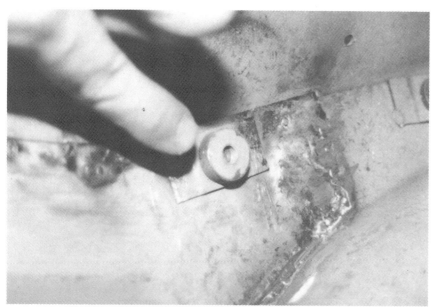

The front and rear wings are bolted to captive nuts fitted to the inner wings (top) and these should be cleared with a suitable tap before bolting the wings in place. Alignment of the lower front edges of the wings and the front of the shroud must be checked and the front panel tried for fit (right and below).

The join at the front of the door may need some filler to adjust. The steel body can be lead loaded.

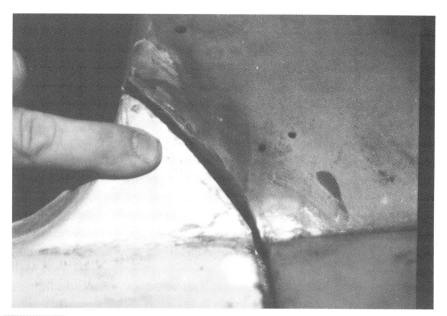

Windscreen captive nuts. Care must be taken to use packing when fitting the windscreen to make sure the frame is not distorted as this will crack the glass.

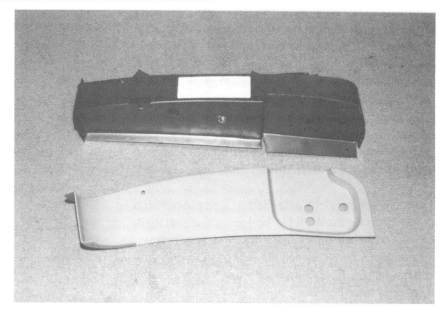

The rear door pillars and cover plates on the coupe differ from those of the roadster.

straightening before they are welded to the new panel. The boot floor is likewise often damaged, mainly because of water leaks from round the boot lid. Various panels are available ranging from the complete floor to part sections. It is much easier to repair this area with the body removed from the chassis.

The inner rear wings also often require replacement and panels to repair these are available. The spot welds holding the inner wings to the rear deck panel will have to be drilled out. When replacing these care must be taken to maintain the correct profile for the bolt holes for the rear wings. Once again a template showing these holes is a great advantage.

The inner sill and door pillar assembly (F section) can be purchased either as separate components or as a complete unit. I suppose having the parts already assembled does reduce the work needed and should ensure the correct door aperture. Whichever route is taken the problem of ensuring that the sill is mounted in the right position is the same and the best advice I can give is to say that it should be lightly fixed in place first, all fits checked, and then the rest of the welding done. The inner sill closing panel is welded to the front and rear inner wings as well as to the inner sill. The sill sealing panel, which rests on top of the chassis, is also welded in place at this stage. There are triangular bracing pieces welded between the rear door post and the inner wing.

The outer sill often needs adjustment to make is fit snugly. Only fit this with the door in place so that an even door gap can be maintained along the whole length of the sill. This part of the body is very prominent on the finished car and it is well worth taking the trouble to get the sill fitting well before finally fixing it in place.

Most new wings are supplied without the bolt holes cut and the position of these have to be marked through the inner wing holes. To provide some adjustment the original holes were slotted laterally and once holes have been marked and drilled they should be opened out with a file or a punch if one is available.

There is often difficulty obtaining enough gap between the door and the inner sill for the door rubber seal to fit. Check this when fitting the wings and, if necessary, introduce packing between the rear of the front wing and the panel in front of the door pillar, where the wing fixes with three bolts.

Trial fit the wings to check door gaps. There are a number of captive nuts fitted to the wings and these will need to be welded in place after their position has been ascertained. Positions of the first few holes are marked, working from the end of the wing nearest to the door, and drilled out. The wing is then re-fitted and the next few holes marked and drilled. After another trial fit the remainder of the holes are drilled, in stages. The wing may prove to be too long or slightly differently shaped and it will have to be bent to maintain the correct profile as work proceeds. In extreme cases it may be necessary to cut the flange and then weld it back together after bending the wing. If the wing is over long the edge may need trimming to line up with the other body panels.

When fitting the wing it is important to achieve a nice even fit against the body to hold the wing piping snugly. The whole body must be fully assembled, and all the gaps and the fit of the wing piping checked before it is dismantled for final finishing and painting.

Parts often missing from restored MGAs are the sill finishing strips, fitted from chassis 19949, that should be fitted to cover the line of fixing bolts for the front and rear wings. These finishing strips were originally painted the same colour as the body.

Incidentally, if restoring a Twin Cam, remember that there were some body differences. The access panels in the front inner wings, for example, and also the front duct panel which is shorter on the Twin Cam.

CHAPTER FIVE

ENGINE

The engine fitted to the MGA was the basic BMC 'B' Series unit developed from the original Austin design used in the A40. It is strong and reliable with few real weaknesses and working on it, or carrying out a full rebuild, presents few difficulties.

Before going into rebuilding in detail I have listed below the major changes made by the factory during production which have been taken from the parts lists.

Although the major part of this chapter deals with the pushrod engine, a section at the end deals with the problems that may be encountered with the Twin Cam unit.

1500 (15GB type - low starter motor)
Numbers 101 - 51767

259 Timing chain tensioner added.
3511 Main bearings modified.
5504 Round ends of pushrods enlarged and tappets modified. (Interchangeable with earlier type in sets.)
8570 Different design of connecting rods and caps introduced (only exchange with earlier type as complete matched sets).
16226 Clutch plate cover modified with stronger springs fitted to pressure plate.
17061 Diameter of the dynamo pulley reduced to increase speed of dynamo and thus output. Shorter fan belt needed.

38484 Pistons and gudgeon pins modified.
46342 (plus 46045 to 46100) oil pump, strainer and pick-up modified.

1500 (15GD type - high mounted starter motor - toe board modified to suit - fitted from car number 61504).
Numbers 101 - 7816

6530 Modified connecting rod bearings fitted.

1600 (16GA type).
Numbers 101 - 31660

20846 Exhaust valves made from improved material fitted.
21705 Stronger connecting rods and modified bearing caps fitted (interchange with earlier type only as complete matched sets).

1600 Mark II (16GC type)
Numbers 101 - 8851

2327 (and engine numbers 2157 to 2225). Oil gallery plugs changed. Only one type fitted in place of the two fitted previously.
3708 Modified flywheel fitted.
8263 Timing chain cover modified to accept rubber type of oil seal. Front pulley and oil thrower also modified.

BEFORE ANY WORK STARTS

If there has been a chance to drive the car then the condition of the engine would have become apparent. Any signs of oil smoke from the exhaust, overheating, undue clatter or poor performance should have been noticed. Condition of the valves and cylinder bores can be checked without dismantling by doing a compression test with the plugs removed. The readings at cranking speed for each of the cylinders can be compared and the test repeated with the piston rings sealed with some oil inserted down the plug holes. A wide variation between the readings after the first test indicates some wear or damage to valves or seats and differences between first and second readings, after oil has been added, is indicative of excessive ring clearance due to bore wear or broken rings.

If the engine seems sound, and there is no wish to strip it down just for the sake of it, then just thoroughly flush it out with flushing oil and then clean the sump and filter housing of any sediment and leave well alone. However, if time is available perhaps all the core plugs should be removed and the waterways cleared out and the bearings looked at for sign of wear. In any event, whilst it is out of the car, the clutch plate should be replaced and the whole engine looked at for signs of oil or water leaks.

DISMANTLING THE ENGINE

There are a few rules to observe when dismantling any engine. The first, and most important, is to always use the correct tools for the job. If the correct 1 1/16 AF socket is not available to undo the crankshaft pulley nut then go and borrow or buy one and DO NOT resort to using a heavy hammer and chisel! Likewise make sure the spanners and sockets used fit the nuts and bolts properly. To remove the main bearing caps a slide puller with a 1/2" UNF thread is necessary - separating the bearings with a chisel is not recommended. When using the slide puller, ensure that it is screwed fully into the tapped threads. It is all too easy to strip the threads if it is only screwed in a few turns and removal of the bearing housing will then be very difficult.

Have some sort of note book available to make notes of any parts needed or to note the position of components that will have been forgotten by the time the engine is re-assembled. Have some bags and boxes ready for keeping the small part in. The push rods, valves, cam followers, etc. will need to be kept in order if they are to be re-used so some sort of numbered storage will have to be provided. When writing labels for components use pencil rather than felt tip pens as these can fade.

Firstly make sure that the engine is empty - a sump full of oil will make quite a mess on the workshop floor. Remove the carburettors and put on one side for reconditioning if necessary. When removing the carburettors. look at the heat shield - this will usually have stress cracks round the bolt holes and should be replaced as repairs never last long.

Remove the exhaust manifold (note position of the plate giving the firing order and tappet clearances) and examine the studs that hold the exhaust pipe to the manifold. Often one or more of these are either broken or damaged and will have to be removed and replaced. Broken studs will have to be drilled out.

Remove the rest of the ancillary equipment. The starter motor and dynamo - look at the dynamo adjusting bracket as this is often cracked. The distributor is best removed by undoing the two bolts holding the mounting plate and taking the whole thing out as a unit. Wear in the distributor bearings can easily be checked by testing the shaft for side play. Worn bearings can be replaced but they must be reamed in line after fitting. The external oil pipe is removed and the oil filter. Look at the oil filter to see if all the components are present and correctly assembled. All too often parts are missing and I have seen filters where the metal plate is absent and the filter element is just 'floating around' in the bowl. If the filter is incorrectly assembled it will not be doing the job properly and may, indeed, not be filtering the oil at all! Note that there are two large sealing rings - one in the block and one in the filter head assembly.

Next remove the side cover plates and breather pipe. Note the spacer washer under the bracket for the breather pipe. The overflow pipes for the carburettor bowls are also fixed by a clip to the same stud.

Remove fan and water pump. All rubber hoses should be discarded and replaced with new ones. If the engine has not been run and the condition of the water pump is unknown it is better to replace it with a new one. If the seals have failed the pump usually spins very freely with no resistance. Rebuild kits are available but sometimes problems arise when the old pump is of unknown manufacture - possible a pattern replacement

With the carburettors removed (above) any cracks in the heat shield can be seen. Replacement is the only answer. The inlet and exhaust manifolds are removed noting the positions of the firing order plate and the bracket. Exhaust pipe securing studs are often broken and need drilling out (left and below).

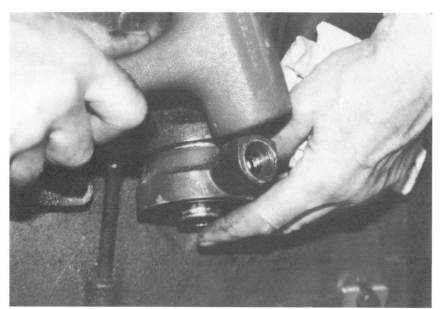

The oil filter top housing. There are sealing rings above and below the housing. Note the use of a 'soft' hammer.

The sensor for the water temperature gauge is often damaged and earlier attempts at removal will have left a mess like this. Once the head is removed then careful work with penetrating oil will often release it. Care must be taken not to damage the threads in the head if it is drilled out.

The water pump should be replaced if there is any doubt about its condition - it is annoying to have to do this after the engine is installed. Always check a new pump to see it fits well and that all the bolt holes line up as some 'pattern' pumps are not accurately cast.

The rev. counter drive is removed. If the engine is not originally from an MGA, and has no provision for the drive, the block can be machined to take one.

When removing the rocker shaft take care it isn't bent by the pressure of the springs on the opened valves - work along slackening all the nuts a turn at a time allowing the shaft to rise parallel to the head until the pressure is released.

The MGA rocker shaft mounting blocks are aluminium and they can distort as seen here. Replace with steel MGB type.

The push rods and cam followers must be stored in order if they are to be reused. Examine the followers for wear or pitting. Replace all the followers as a matter of course if the camshaft is ground or replaced. (above and right). Locking two nuts on a stud will usually allow it to be extracted easily. Any damaged or rusty studs must be replaced (below).

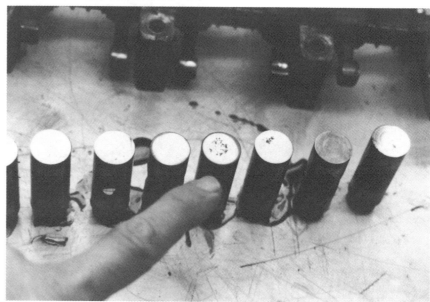

at some time - so it is probably best to just fit a new pump.

Remove the rev. counter drive. Incidentally, if the engine is not an MGA unit and comes, for example, from a Z Magnette then the block may not be drilled for this drive. However, a good machine shop will be able to drill and machine the block to take the drive.

Before much more dismantling takes place, loosen the front pulley nut after knocking back the lock washer. A 1 5/16 AF socket and a long bar are necessary and the flywheel will need to be jammed. As assistant with a tyre lever or large screwdriver blade held against the starter ring gear will suffice.

Remove the rocker cover - over tightened cover nuts may have distorted this over the years and some straightening, or perhaps searching for a better replacement, may be needed. However, it is worth having a cover in good condition as it is a very noticeable part of the engine bay.

Remove the rocker shaft - to avoid bending it loosen the nuts next to closed valves first. Examine the shaft and the rocker arms for wear. The rocker shaft pedestals on MGA engines are usually made of aluminium and it is worth looking out for a set from an MGB engine which are cast iron - make sure they are the correct pattern as those on the later MGB engine had a different rear pillar.

Remove the push rods and camshaft followers, keeping these in order. Examine for wear. Any followers exhibiting wear should be discarded and certainly should be renewed if the camshaft is being ground or replaced.

Remove cylinder head nuts - reverse order to the tightening sequence shown in the manual - and remove the head. Sometimes water seepage from the water jacket adjacent to the studs may corrode these to the head. Very careful use of a soft hammer on the side of the head can help as well as penetrating oil round the studs. Resist the temptation to force anything between the head and block as this is usually unnecessary and may cause damage.

With the head lifted away the studs can be removed. Use either a stud remover or lock together two nuts on the stud and wind the stud out of the block. Any stud that is damaged or badly corroded must be replaced. If any work is to be done on the block the engine number plate should also be removed. This plate is secured by two hard steel rivets with spiral shanks. To remove these gently prize up the underside of the aluminium plate and once the rivets start to move a couple of screwdriver blades under the edge will usually lift them out. The rivets can be re-used although replacements are available. If the head comes off a rivet then the remainder should be punched down the hole into the block as far as possible and a shortened new rivet used to replace the plate.

Remove the clutch, releasing the holding bolts progressively, which will reveal the state of the flywheel face. If this is badly worn it may need re-facing.

Turning to the front of the engine, remove the previously loosened front nut and the front pulley (being careful as it is fragile). If the rivets are loose then the pulley needs replacing. Look for wear in the face where the seal rubs. The felt seal on the MGA cover can be replaced by the early MGB rubber seal provided an appropriate cover is found. The oil thrower must also be replaced with the later, flatter thrower used with the rubber seal.

Remove the timing chain cover (note that the washers under the bolt heads are oval to spread the load) and the timing chain tensioner. The tensioner usually wears and can be replaced as a unit. Before removing the timing chain, remove the bolt securing the camshaft sprocket to the camshaft - again preventing the camshaft and crankshaft turning by jamming the flywheel. Lever off the timing chain sprockets and chain.. Incidentally it is easy to forget the small gasket behind the timing chain tensioner when re-assembling the engine.

Remove the camshaft thrust plate. On the MGA this usually has a white metal face which can be worn quite badly but the MGB bronze faced thrust plate can be used to replace it. Remove the flywheel. With this out of the way the back plate can be removed. Note that the holding bolts on the back plate either have their heads reduced in thickness to clear the flywheel or are recessed into holes in the plate. Some engines have locking tabs, not lock washers, and some back plates are thinner than others. The plate locates on two dowels.

The engine can then be inverted - taking care to protect the top face of the block. The sump pan, oil pick-up, strainer and oil pump can be removed. The oil pump should be replaced as a matter of course unless it is

The front pulley must be examined to see if the rivets are tight and also that the surface the seal runs on is smooth.

Examine the timing chain tensioner for wear. Complete replacement assemblies are available.

In this picture (taken from above) the removal of the camshaft drive sprockets is achieved with the use of two tyre levers.

The camshaft thrust plate is often worn. Replacement MGB type are available.

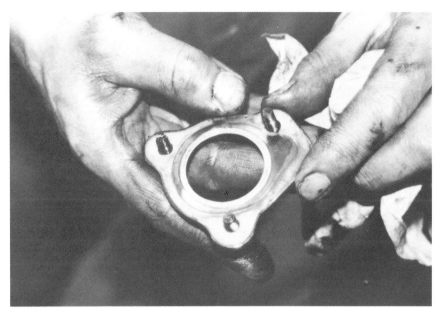

If the starter ring gear is badly worn then it will need replacing before the flywheel is balanced. New rings are heated and shrunk on to the flywheel.

If the engine has done a high mileage then the oil pump may be worn. Packing a new pump with grease will help it prime.

Removing the big end caps will reveal the state of the bearings. It is essential to keep the caps with the correct conrod. If they are not marked use number punches to stamp the cap and rod.

The pistons and rods are pushed out from the bottom.

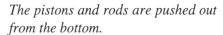

A slide puller is used here to remove the main bearing caps. The puller must be screwed well into the tapping in the cap.

known to be fairly new. The big end bearing caps are then undone and the engine placed on it s side for the pistons and rods to be pushed out of the top of the block. Keep all the bearing caps in order and if they are not numbered (NOTE that the rods are handed and offset - nos. 1 & 3 and 2 & 4 are the same pattern) then number them with number punches. With the pistons and rods removed turn the engine back upside down.

The main bearing cap holding nuts are removed and a slide hammer with a 1/2 UNF thread is used to remove the caps. Try to obtain the correct tool for this operation as the 'heavy hammer' approach will damage the bearing caps. The crankshaft can now be lifted clear.

Once they have been removed from the block separate the pistons from the conrods. To do this without damage, hold the piston in a vice by inserting suitable plugs into each end of the gudgeon pin and clamp up on these (3/8 in. Allen head bolts usually do the job). Use a socket to undo the gudgeon pin clamp bolt.

Remove the distributor drive and then the camshaft - taking care not to damage the bearing surfaces if they are not going to be renewed. The MGA camshaft can be replaced by an MGB camshaft provided the end is turned down and a keyway cut for the rev. counter drive. Remove the oil pump studs before turning the block back the right way up. Incidentally it is easier when replacing a camshaft to stand the block on the rear plate and lower the shaft downwards - the bearings are easily damaged.

INSPECTION AND MACHINING

Establishing the degree of wear is not easy without access to the correct measuring tools and having the knowledge to use them. If uncertain the best course is to take the parts to a machine shop to have them measured for wear. Bore wear is fairly easily seen and if any appreciable ridge can be felt at the top of the bores then a re-bore is probably needed. Examination of the marks on the top of the piston will show if the bores are standard or have been taken out to an oversize. If the engine has already been bored to maximum oversize then it will have to be sleeved. Bear in mind that not every oversize of piston may be available and the new pistons should be obtained before any machining is carried out. In any event it is better for the machinist to have the new pistons available to check their dimensions when boring the engine.

A word here about having machining work done is not out of place. Many engines have been damaged by poor machining and before entrusting work to a company try to find out if they are used to working on 'B' Series engines and, if possible, go on personal recommendation. If uncertain about which company to use perhaps a word with the M.G. specialist supplier selling the pistons, etc. may help as they often have a firm they use and can recommend. It may even be better to route the work through them so you have someone to shout at if things go wrong!

Anyway returning to the engine and examining it for wear. If the bores are worn then forget about the pistons as these will need replacing anyway. If the bores are good then look at the pistons and rings carefully. Do not damage the surface of the pistons removing the carbon - soaking in oil or paraffin will soften this. The rings must not be broken or seized in the slots. New ring sets are sometimes available and these often have the top ring stepped so they clear any slight ridges left at the top of the bores by the old rings.

Replacement rings must be checked in the bores and the ends carefully filed if they do not have sufficient gap - the correct figures are in the workshop manual. The bores will need 'glaze busting' before the new rings are fitted to help them bed in.

Now examine the crankshaft and bearings. I would advocate always replacing the bearings but only have the crank reground if necessary. The condition of the bearing surfaces of the crankshaft can be examined and measured for any sign of ovality - if in doubt consult an expert. Any signs of pitting or ridges on the surface can need correcting by a re-grind. Once again the final result will only be as good as the machinist carrying out the work. A crank ground with worn tools will often not have the correct radii at the corners of the journal. A badly radiused journal can create a weak point in the crankshaft leading to breakage. Make sure that all the oilways in the crank are clear after machining. It is worth considering having any crank crack tested and particularly one from the 1588cc engine. This crank is for some reason prone to cracking and often an earlier 1500 crank will have been incorrectly substituted.

If the crankshaft main bearings have worn badly then the crankshaft will have run against the face of the rear main bearing cap. The oil seal here relies on the gap between the face of the lip on the cap, and the block, and the scroll on the rear of the crankshaft. If these are worn serious oil leaks can result and the only cure is a new crankshaft and for the block and bearing cap to be built up and re-bored to the correct size. If the scroll on the crankshaft is not too badly worn then just the building up and re-machining of the housing may suffice.

The camshaft and cam followers should be examined and if worn replaced as a set.

CLEANING ALL PARTS

The block should have all the core plugs, oil gallery plugs, cam bearings and studs removed and then it can be cleaned in a caustic bath to remove the paint and all the oil and sludge. Most machine shops dealing with engine work will have suitable equipment. This caustic solution will dissolve any aluminium component and also the white metal bearings for the camshaft which is why they must be removed before dipping. For the same reason make sure the engine number plate is removed as described earlier. The caustic solution will not, however, remove the scale from waterways and this should be carefully chipped out where possible.

When the block is returned after machining check that all the oilways are clear before the engine is re-assembled. If there is any delay before the engine is to be worked on ensure it is protected from any surface rusting.

The cylinder head should also be cleaned of paint and oil. Both the top of the block and the face of the head must be checked and trued up by skimming - make sure this is done carefully and that only the minimum of metal is removed.

The rest of the engine components are best cleaned with a solution such as 'Jizer' and examined to make sure all oilways, etc. are clear.

The connecting rods must be examined to ensure they are not damaged. The bore size of the bearing housing must be checked - the correct sizes are given in the manual. If the shells have been run until they are worn badly then the surface of the bearing housing in the rods may be polished and worn. If oversize, the caps can be machined and the housing re-bored to correct size. The rods will then certainly then need to be balanced as a set.

ASSEMBLING THE ENGINE

The process of assembling an engine is very straightforward but if a reliable unit is to result then great care must be taken at all stages.

The golden rule is cleanliness. This applies not just to the exterior of the components of the engine but, more importantly, to the condition of the internal oilways and oil feeds. As we have seen when considering the machining work, all of this must be checked afterwards to see that no residue was left in any oilways or drillings. Obviously a clean and dust free area to assemble the engine will be needed.

A word now about joint sealers and "instant gaskets". Modern product are good and are very oil resistant and it is this very quality that has ruined many an engine. Any surplus sealant that is separated from a joint within the engine can very easily become lodged in an oilway and, as it will not dissolve in the oil, could starve a bearing. I have seen an engine where all the valve gear was starved of oil because a blob of gasket sealer had blocked the oil feed to the head. The rule is that "more is not necessarily better" so only apply sufficient sealer for the purpose and never too much.

Although all the machining may have been carried out by a competent firm, mistakes do happen and as the engine is assembled check all clearances of bearings, rings etc. Particularly, as each main bearing is tightened check that the crankshaft will still revolve freely. Likewise check as each big end bearing is assembled. If in doubt, trial assemble each rod on the crankshaft before assembling the engine to check it is free when tightened up. Check crankshaft end float carefully and adjust thrust washers - remembering to assemble them correctly. Check the camshaft timing and adjust with off-set keys if necessary.

Always use an assembly paste, like 'Lubriplate' to protect the bearings when the engine is first started and try to turn the engine over enough times on the starter to bring up the oil pressure before it is fired up. Packing the oil pump with grease - such as Castrol LM - will help it prime.

If the engine has had the block and head skimmed always check the piston height and valve clearance. Remember that the studs and nuts must not be rusty or damaged or the torque wrench readings will be

Before the block is cleaned in caustic solution it is advisable to remove the engine number plate. This is done by prising up the rivets. If a head breaks off a rivet the remainder should be punched down into the hole and a shortened new rivet fitted. These special rivets are hardened and have a spiral 'thread'.

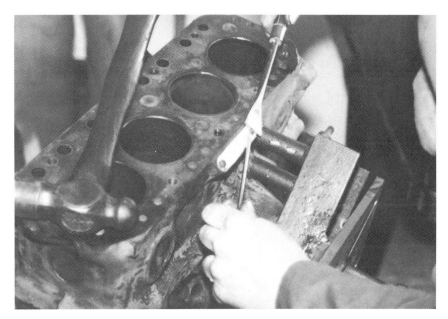

Re-ground crankshaft, rods, pistons etc. await assembly. Provided all measurements have been checked and all parts thoroughly cleaned, careful assembly will ensure a long lasting engine (below left). The sump, rocker cover, etc. are cleaned ready to receive primer and enamel paint (below right).

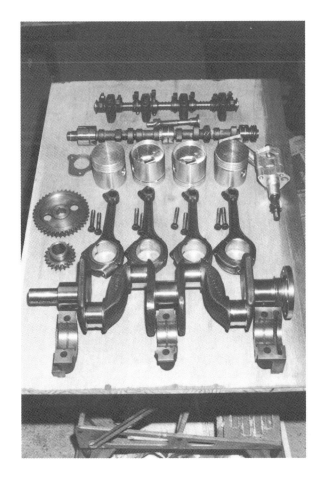

Crankshaft end float is measured here with a dial gauge. Correctly there should be 0.002 in. - 0.003 in. end float. When assembling the thrust washers note that the workshop manual in most editions gave the wrong instructions - the oil grooves should face AWAY from the bearing and towards the crankshaft not as stated in the manual.

The piston ring gap is checked with a feeler gauge (below left). A piston ring clamp is used to fit the pistons. Oil the rings to help them slide into the bore and never use too much force as replacement rings are hard to find (below right).

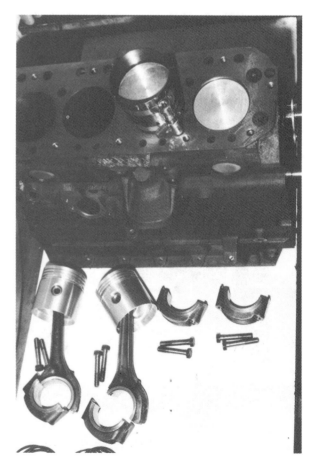

CHECKING THE CAMSHAFT TIMING

When assembling the engine, particularly with a new or re-ground camshaft, it is a good idea to check the camshaft timing. There is always the possibility that the camshaft has been ground slightly out of true with the keyway and some adjustment will be needed for the engine to give full performance. If the engine is to be used seriously in competition this process is essential.

To carry out the check, a dial gauge with a suitable magnetic clamp and a degree wheel will be needed. The degree wheel in the photograph was produced by one of the manufacturers of performance camshafts. With number one piston set at top dead centre, the dial gauge is first mounted on the front of the crankshaft and held by the starter dog so that the TDC mark is opposite a fixed point. The easiest way to provide this fixed point is to trap a length of stiff wire under a convenient bolt head and bend one end over the edge of the degree wheel so that it lines up with the marked scale. The dial gauge is first set up to check this TDC position by taking a reading from the top face of the piston at, say 0.050in. before and 0.050in. after TDC. Noting these readings on the dial and re-setting the TDC on the dial to exactly half way between the two readings will give an accurate position for it.

With one of the pushrods in place for the inlet valve on number one piston set up the dial gauge to take a reading from it. What you need to find is the point at which the valve is fully open. Let us take the example of a standard MGA engine:- The workshop manual gives us figures for the inlet valve opening of 16 degrees before top dead centre and closing 56 degrees after bottom dead centre, that means the valve is open for 252 degrees. Dividing this figure by two and deducting the 16 degrees before TDC from the result gives a figure of 110 degrees after TDC for the point of full lift.

Now readings are taken from the camshaft using the dial gauge at, say, 0.050in. before and after the point of maximum lift - noting the readings on the degree wheel. Once again dividing the number of degrees between the two readings in half will give an accurate figure. If the reading differs from specification (in this case 110 degrees) then this will need adjustment. For a race engine then it should be within a degree but for a road engine one would only get seriously concerned if the error was over 3-4 degrees. Adjustment is made by filing up an oversized key to off set the sprocket from the camshaft. The crankshaft sprocket key (2H326) is suitable as it is thicker. Adjustable sprockets are available but these are expensive and are really only for serious competition where some degree of adjustment may be needed for experimentation.

inaccurate and components, like the cylinder head, will not be sufficiently tightened down.

Once an engine has been fully assembled remember to paint the edges of the gaskets the same colour as the rest of the engine. The engines originally were painted after they were assembled.

All rebuilt engines must be carefully "run in" and it is much better to do this over a short period. Too many rebuilt cars do just a few hundred miles a year and any problems that arise are usually well outside any sort of guarantees given with components purchased.

THE TWIN CAM ENGINE

So far we have only considered the pushrod engine in this chapter. The Twin Cam engine is a completely different prospect for the amateur restorer and although the process of dismantling and examination of components is not a lot different from the standard engine it really does need a considerable amount of specialist knowledge to make sure that it is correctly checked and assembled to give a long period of reliable use. For this reason, as well as a lack of space, I do not propose here to go into any great detail on the processes involved. Anyone brave enough to tackle the job on their own probably does not need any advice from me! Remember that if you do take the engine to a specialist make sure he does know the Twin Cam well. Of recent years many heads have been ruined by people skimming them to try to cure leaks and end up with the valves too close to the pistons.

For reliability the engine should use low compression pistons unless it is built up specifically for racing. There are still a number of sets of the high compression pistons around but do not be tempted to use these. The later cylinder head with the steel inserts is a must, or the earlier head modified, and the later, longer tappet buckets, valve springs and shim retainers must be used, This modification by the factory was to stop the early

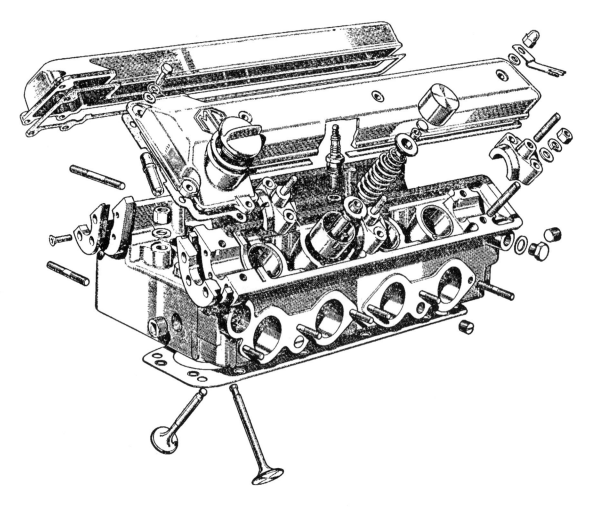

The Twin Cam head.

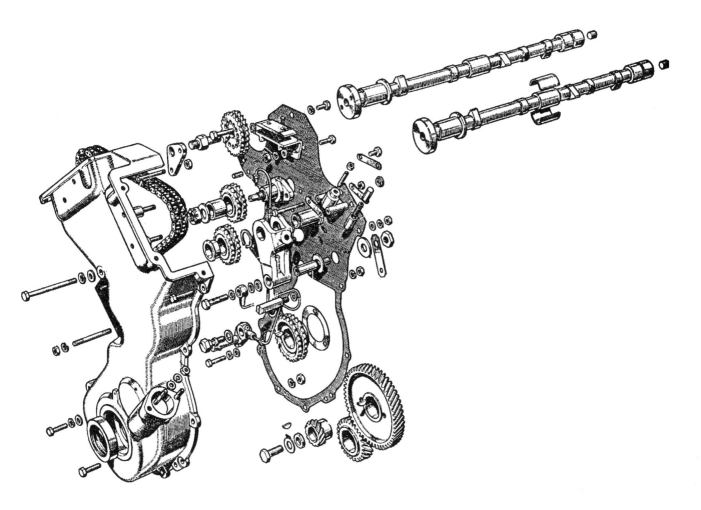

The Twin Cam chain drive (above) and half speed shaft (below).

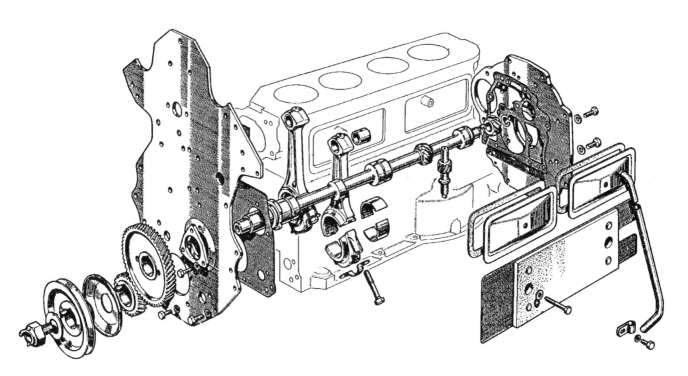

The Twin Cam head often suffers from being over skimmed or badly skimmed. There are four bosses cast into the head which are used to locate the casting when machining - setting it up from any other points can result in it being machined out of square.

In this picture the depth of the combustion chamber is tested with a purpose made gauge. If too much metal has been removed then the valves may touch the pistons.

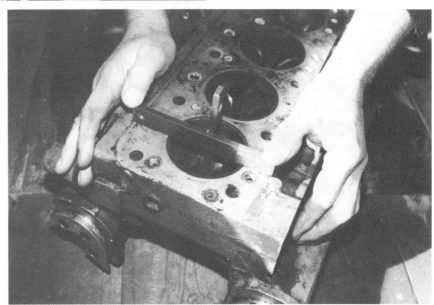

Compare this picture with the one on the next page to see the difference between early and late heads.

MGA RESTORATION GUIDE

A late Twin Cam head with the steel inserts. The picture on page 80 shows an early head that has suffered damage when one of the short tappet buckets has turned and jammed in the housing.

Three tappet buckets. On the left is the last factory version with a longer skirt and a chamfer on the top edge. The central one is a new part which has been nitrided to reduce wear, and the last is the early short bucket.

Low and high compression pistons. The high compression piston on the right of the picture is best left for competition use. Some new low compression pistons have been made by Peter Wood with a reduced height crown to help give sufficient valve clearance when heads have been over skimmed.

The early type of Twin Cam rod compared to the later type with the 'hammer head' shape to the little end boss.

All crankshafts, both Twin Cam and pushrod, must be crack tested. This 1600 crankshaft proved to be badly cracked although to the naked eye it appeared perfect.

This ruined crankshaft is the outcome of poor grinding with an incorrectly shaped tool. There is no radius at the outer edges of the bearing surface - causing a weakness that will lead to early failure.

shorter tappet buckets tilting and jamming. The earlier shim retainers were of a different pattern and of softer material than the later type, introduced with the modified valve springs. The early type can wear and end up tight against the inside of the tappet bucket, making the shim adjustment superfluous.

The crankshafts should not be ground too far and must be crack tested. For reliability it should be no more than 20, or at most 30 thou. undersized. But more important the radii at the sides of the journal must be maintained and the machining must be of a very high standard. Experts recommend that the crankshaft be tuftrided as some of the reticular tin bearings now available will wear the crank journals at very low mileages. The original bearings were copper/lead, indium infused and these are preferable if they can be located.

When an engine is assembled there are a few points it is very important to note. Firstly the rear crankshaft oil seal must be a good fit in the housing but it must not be too tight. A considerable amount of time should be spent working on the seal to make it fit well. If it is left too large for the housing it can split it, and also the heat build up at the seal can overheat the crankshaft, which will then have to be scrapped. The shaft must be capable of being rotated freely by hand with the main bearings nuts tightened down to their correct torque setting. As the bearing housings need to be removed a number of times during this operation, consider making a bridge puller for them rather than using the sliding hammer tool.

When assembling the big ends check the bolt lengths carefully first to ensure that they are not too long and are "bottoming out" in the rods - this may either strip the threads or crack the rods. It goes without saying that the rods should be of the later type if possible and that they should be crack tested and balanced. The journal size should be checked to ensure the correct bearing nip - dimensions are given in the manual.

With the bottom end assembled, the piston height must be checked to make sure there is enough clearance for the valves. There are some of the lower compression pistons sets available with the head height reduced to help gain enough clearance.

When dismantling or assembling the valve gear take note of the workshop manual instructions about lifting out the camshafts. The bearing cap nuts must be loosened progressively, a turn at a time starting from the rear bearing, to allow the camshaft to rise evenly. If the camshaft is raised at one end damage to the camshaft or housing will result. If second-hand tappet buckets are used these MUST be crack tested. The factory range of shims is 86-116 thou. but it is possible to use shims from 78-130 thou. if necessary. The valve seats are cast in place and are often not concentric with the valve guides. Great care is therefore needed when these are replaced - although replacement is not advisable unless absolutely necessary.

When re-cutting seats it is imperative to remove the minimum amount of metal so as not to jeopardise the shim range. Remember that the more the valve is recessed into the head the more the valve stem protrudes through and the less shimming range is available.

The timing chain tensioner must be examined, both for wear and for any stripped threads. It is also vital to pressure test, and clean out if necessary, all the oil feeds that lubricate the chain and sprockets - especially the small bleed holes that feed the chain and the half speed shaft and crankshaft gear wheels.

The Twin Cam engine requires precise settings of valve and ignition timing and of mixture to work efficiently and reliably. When running a car with an engine that has not been stripped and examined, and may possibly be to early specification, then consider that it may be running on "borrowed time". At the very least the valve covers should be removed and the head looked at to see if there are inserts in the tappet bucket housings. If possible the sump should be dropped to see if the later, red painted, crankshaft is fitted and the later rods used.

When setting the carburettors do not aim for a smooth idle. To ensure enough fuel at higher engine speeds, the mixture must be rich at idle. Fuel helps the engine run cool and competition Twin Cams do not do many miles per gallon! If the carburettors are past their best have them rebuilt as worn units cannot be set up to give the correct mixture.

Use the correct spark plugs - Champion N3 or equivalent - and make sure that the later distributor is fitted and that this is not worn. The distributor advance curve must be checked if there is any doubt

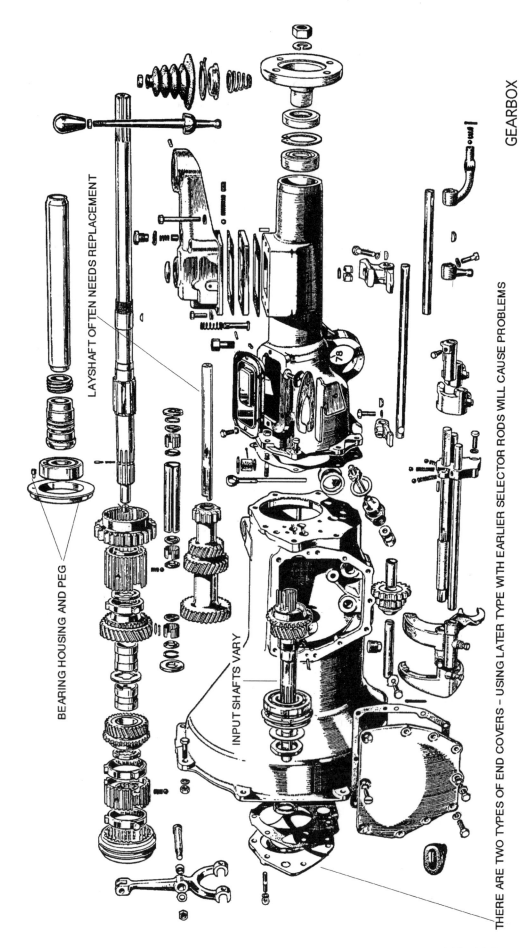

LAYSHAFT OFTEN NEEDS REPLACEMENT

BEARING HOUSING AND PEG

INPUT SHAFTS VARY

GEARBOX

THERE ARE TWO TYPES OF END COVERS – USING LATER TYPE WITH EARLIER SELECTOR RODS WILL CAUSE PROBLEMS

CHAPTER SIX

OTHER MECHANICAL COMPONENTS

GEARBOX

There were quite a few changes made to the MGA gearbox during the production run of the cars. The rear oil seal in the rear extension was changed three times. The oil seal in the front cover assembly was improved and the casing changed three times. To summarise, the changes were:-

REAR EXTENSION
Engine 101 to 743 leather seal 1G 3419
Engine 744 to 10989 seal 11G3147
These two seals are interchangeable
Engine 10990 to 51767 (last engine in 15GB series) seal 1H3339 (now RTC 447)
Engine 15GD101 to end of production. Seal 1H3275

FRONT COVER

From engine 7981 the front cover was modified, earlier cars did not have an oil seal - only an oil return scroll. The later cover with rubber oil seal cannot be fitted to the earlier box without modification as the selector rods will foul the cover.

MAIN CASE.

Up to the introduction of the 15GD type of engine in January 1959, when the starter motor was mounted higher, there were two types of case - the earlier with

UNF threads and the later with UNC threads. From engine number 15GD101 to 16GC4747 the casing was modified to accommodate the higher starter position. On the 1600 Mk II from engine 16GC4748 the casing was strengthened with stiffening ribs and stronger bellhousing.

Because of the variation in the design of the spline on the mainshaft, and the introduction of a flange for the propshaft, not all the types of gearbox are interchangeable. Before purchasing parts for any gearbox it is advisable to check to see if it has been changed during previous ownership of the car. In many cases the original box and propshaft may have been replaced with those of a later pattern.

REBUILDING A GEARBOX.

The MGA gearbox is a simple and sturdy unit but does suffer from wear at higher mileages. Usually this results in extra noise, or slipping out of gear, especially on overrun. If the car has been road tested then some idea of the condition of the gearbox would have been formed and it may only be necessary to give everything a good clean out and renewal of oil seals and gaskets. However, the chances are that some new parts will be needed and the road test may have given the clue as to where to look for wear.

Firstly, if the car jumps out of gear the first place to look

When removing or replacing the main shaft bearing housing it is better to warm the casing rather than just drift it out. When replacing it make sure the dowel is located correctly before the housing cools.

The imput shaft changed from engine number 16GC/H3929 with the number of splines increasing from 10 to 23.

Early and late front covers. The early cover did not have the rubber oil seal but the later cover cannot be fitted to the early gearbox without modification as the recesses for the selector rods are not as deep.

The layshaft usually needs replacing where the gearbox has done a high mileage or where dirty oil or oil of the wrong type has been used.

is the selectors. In most cases this is where the problem lies if the gearbox sounds otherwise quiet. Each selector rod has three slots machined in it to locate the spring loaded fork locating balls. Wear in these slots or of the balls, or a weak spring, can cause the box to slip out of gear. It is also possible that either wear on the forks or an obstruction such as the wrong front cover is to blame.

When stripping the gearbox refer to the workshop manual for the procedure, but to remove the main shaft bearing housing it is better to warm the casing rather than try to drift it out, causing damage. When replacing this, once again warming the casing will help but the locating dowel must be correctly positioned before the casing cools down.

The synchromesh cones will usually be worn and the gears will need to be carefully inspected. New parts are available as well as complete sets of close ratio gears. These were originally offered as an optional extra and cars fitted with these gears carried the engine number prefix 'Da' instead of 'U'. Although a very nice gearbox for competition it does have some disadvantages for road use, especially if the higher 4.1 rear axle ratio of the 1600 Mk II is used, as first gear is then quite high and the clutch needs to be slipped when re-starting on hills.

With the high prices of new components for the gearbox the temptation is to cannibalise parts from other, second hand units and as the internals of many BMC boxes of the period were the same there is a rich source of parts.

However, it is not a good idea to mix gears from different boxes as the wear patterns on these will vary and a very noisy gearbox may result.

The layshaft is often worn quite badly as it suffers from shortage of lubrication - especially if the wrong grade of oil has been used. SAE 30 was the factory recommendation.

It is important that the spigot bearing in the rear of the crankshaft is in good condition and that the clutch plate slides freely on the splines of the input shaft. A tight fit here or corrosion on the splines of the input shaft could cause clutch drag and difficulty in selecting first and reverse gears.

Care must be taken when purchasing parts for the clutch as the number of splines on the input shaft changed from 10 to 23 from engine number 16GC/H3929. It is possible to fit a diaphragm spring clutch but it will probably be necessary to grind away some of the inside of the bell housing to provide clearance.

Whilst on the subject of the clutch it is worth mentioning that if difficulty is experienced engaging gears, especially first and reverse, with the engine running, but not when it is stationary, the problem is that the clutch is not freeing off properly. This may be due to a worn release bearing but before going to all the trouble of taking the engine and gearbox out first check the rest of the system. Because the clutch is released by quite a small amount of movement any lost motion in the system caused by worn clevis pins can be significant.

It is also worth checking the hydraulics as slave cylinders are often difficult to bleed completely. There should be about 3/8th in. of movement at the slave cylinder.

REAR AXLE

Because they seldom give trouble, the temptation with the back axle is just to give it a coat of paint and refit it to the car. If the car has been driven and all seems well then this may be all that is needed but whilst it is out of the car it could be a good idea just to check one or two points.

Firstly, has the axle been damaged in an accident. Because the ends are fixed to the springs, and thus to the chassis, any accident that results in a heavy blow being given to the engine, tending to force the differential backwards, can bend the axle. This distortion will impose loads on the bearings and on the half shafts. Should there by any reason to suspect that this type of accident has occurred then check the alignment of the axle tubes.

Secondly, the half shafts themselves should be examined. As I will mention shortly there are three different types of half shafts for both disc and wire wheeled cars. Excessive wear in the splines, especially noticeable in the early ten spline shafts, and any sign that the half shaft has been bent in an accident means they need replacing and that the bearings, too, are suspect.

Thirdly check the inner hub securing nuts. These must be done up very tight, with a proper socket and a long bar. Failure to do this allows the bearing to move on the machined surface of the axle, causing wear. The flexing loads then applied to the half shaft will cause it to break about half way along its length. Note that from chassis 10917 (disc) and 11450 (wire) the thread on the left hand side of the axle had a left hand thread - turn clockwise to unscrew.

The workshop manual gives good instructions for rebuilding the differential but a dial gauge is necessary, together with some knowledge of the techniques used to measure clearances, backlash, etc. However, that said, the job is fairly straightforward provided the shims of the required thicknesses are obtained. If in doubt don't be afraid to give the differential to a specialist to check the settings.

When replacing the hub bearings they must be a drive fit on the axle tube and in the hub. Using 'quick fixes' like Loctite will seldom be successful if there is much wear on the machined surfaces of the axle and bearing housing. A better solution in the long run is to have the axle ends built up and machined to size. When assembling the bearing and carrier note that on disc wheeled cars there is a spacer between the outer edge of the bearing and the cap on the end of the half shaft to lock the bearing tightly into the housing when the wheel studs are tightened. On wire wheeled cars the rim on the splined hub serves the same purpose.

Because not all replacement parts are made to exactly the same specification as the original it pays to check that the bearing is held tightly with the gaskets in place. To check this; first assemble the hub and bearing carrier without any gaskets and check that there is a clearance between the face of the hub and the bearing carrier. If the gap is greater than the thickness of the gasket supplied then a thicker gasket is needed or silicon 'instant' gasket used. If there is no clearance then shims will have to be made to provide the necessary location for the bearings. Some of the early 1500 axles did not have the additional 'O' ring seal later introduced to reduce the chance of leaks from the hub/bearing carrier joint. Using modern sealers will probably prove sufficient provided it is assembled carefully.

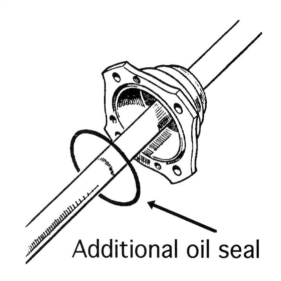

Additional oil seal

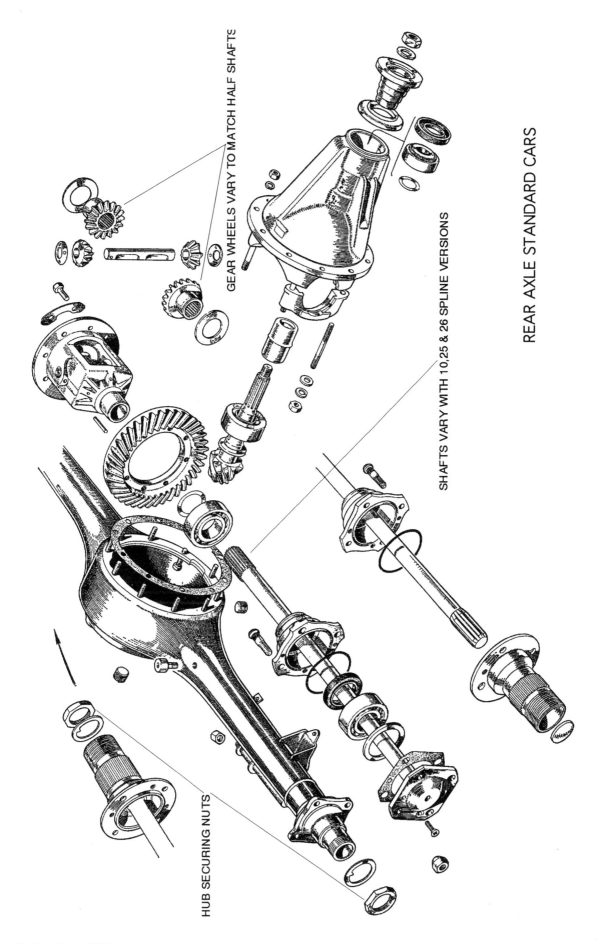

GEAR WHEELS VARY TO MATCH HALF SHAFTS

REAR AXLE STANDARD CARS

SHAFTS VARY WITH 10,25 & 26 SPLINE VERSIONS

HUB SECURING NUTS

Now let us look at those three different types of half shafts. As far as I can tell from an examination of parts lists the situation is as follows:-

1500 and Twin Cams to chassis 2370 were all fitted with axles containing differential gear wheels, and half shafts with ten splines (gear wheels ATB7122, half shafts ATB7206, [wire wheels and Twin Cam], ATD7190 [disc wheels 1500]).

1600 to chassis 82892 (disc wheels) and 82748 (wire wheels) and Twin Cams from chassis 2371 were fitted with axles that had *twenty six* spline gear wheels and half shafts. (gear wheels ATB7282, half shafts ATB7279[disc wheels] ATB7386 [wire wheels]). From chassis 8293 (disc wheels) and 82749 (wire wheels) and all 1600 Mk II's they all had *twenty five* spline gear wheels and axles (gear wheels BTB150, half shafts BTB151[disc wheels] and BTB153 [wire wheels]).

The moral here is to count the splines carefully when ordering replacements as a *twenty five* spline shaft will fit in a *twenty six* spline differential but will fail under load. At the time of writing 10, 25 and 26 spline half shafts are available but only 10 and 25 spline gear wheels. The 25 spline gears are the same as those used in early MGB's.

Half shafts need to be pressed into the hubs and should need a 5 - 10 ton pressure. Once again do not accept any loosely fitting shafts as these will soon fail in use. There is a welsh plug in the hub to seal against oil leakage. As with core plugs, these need a couple of sharp blows to spread them to secure them in place.

CARBURETTORS

The pushrod cars were fitted with twin S.U. H4 carburettors of 1 1/2in. diameter and the Twin Cam with twin S.U. HD6 of 1 3/4in. diameter. The needle sizes on the pushrod cars were changed when the 1600 model was introduced - the 1500 had AUD1222 GS needles and the 1600 and Mk II AUD1005 6 needles. The Twin Cam was fitted with AUD1276 OA6 needles. Both types of carburettor use the AUC 4387 damper springs but the damper on the Twin Cam and 1600s was AUC 8114 and the 1500 AUC 8103.

REBUILDING

The temptation with carburettors is to just give them a clean up and refit, especially if nearing the end of a long rebuild. However, unless their condition is known it is important to, at least, check them over as past owners often will have 'messed about' with them and may have changed their specification.

All the parts, and even complete new carburettors for the pushrod cars, are available from specialists, such as Burlen Fuel Services in Salisbury or S.U. Midel Pty. Ltd. in Australia, or from the usual M.G. parts suppliers. There are rebuilding services available but these are not cheap and as the carburettors are easy to work on I suggest that most people will have little difficulty provided the correct rebuild kits are purchased.

The first job is to clean the carburettors externally using a carburettor cleaner. Always wear rubber gloves and work outside and avoid inhaling the fumes from this cleaner. A small brush, like a toothbrush, will help free stubborn grime. When carburettors are overhauled professionally then bead blasting or ultrasonic cleaning is used but a quite acceptable job can be done by hand.

Remove any banjo bolts and fuel pipes. All flexible fuel pipes must be discarded, unless they are nearly new. The rubber inner pipes perish and good replacements are available - search out those with the correct pattern of end clamping. Remove the filters and springs from the inlet pipe to the float chamber bowls.

Mark the suction chamber and carburettor body so they can later be replaced in the same relative position. Remove the piston dampers and, after removing the screws, lift off the suction chamber. The spring and piston can now be lifted off carefully and any oil in the top of the piston drained off. The needle locking screw is then loosened and the needle removed. Look to see what reference code is stamped on the shank.

Dependent on how far it is intended to strip them down, remove all the linkages ensuring you remember how they fit together. Look for any signs of wear in clevis pins, etc.

Pull the jet downwards and unscrew the jet adjusting nut and spring. Unscrew the locking nut and withdraw the whole assembly carefully. Lift off the upper jet bearing and copper washer and extract the gland and gland washer. After removing the gland spring, withdraw the lower jet bearing from the locking nut, noting the position of the thin brass washer. Withdraw

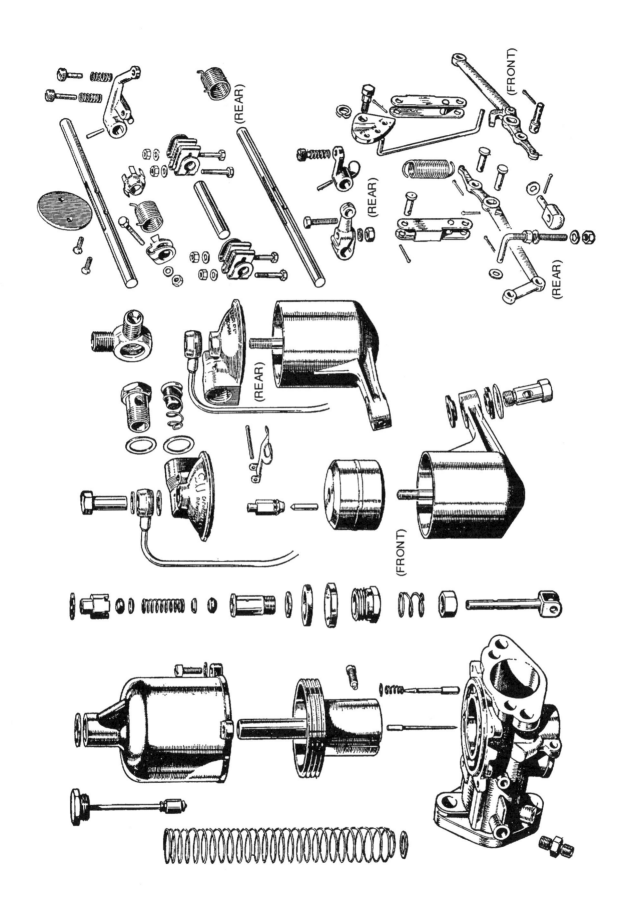

(REAR)

(FRONT)

(REAR)

(REAR)

(REAR)

(REAR)

(FRONT)

the gland and brass gland washer from inside the bearing.

Disconnect the float chamber from the carburettor body by removing the bolt. Mark the relative positions of the chamber and lid and remove the bolt holding the lid to the chamber and remove the overflow pipe and washers. Note that the washer with cut-outs fits below the drain pipe and the plain washer above. Remove the float.

Push out the hinge pin in the lid (this only comes out one way - push on the end opposite to the splines on the shaft). With the pin removed, lift off the fork and extract the needle valve - care do not discard or damage this valve if it is the original metal type. The valve seating is removed using a small socket spanner.

The replacement valves found in most kits now have plastic type of needle valves. I have found these more prone to cause fuel starvation when under bonnet temperatures are high - perhaps because the pressure build up in the float chamber when the fuel vaporises forces them shut. For this reason I have found the metal type better or have fitted the ball type 'Gros Jet' valves. If re-using the old valves check that the conical face of the needle isn't worn. I have managed to carefully reface these on a modellers lathe.

Now is the time to examine the throttle spindle for wear. When used for high mileages the bearing surface in the carburettor body becomes worn and air will leak down the sides of the shaft. The wear will also not allow the throttle butterfly disc to mate correctly with the inner surface of the body.

It is easier to look for this wear with the return spring removed from the throttle spindle, so slacken off the clamping bolt and the bolt on the operating lever and remove these. Look to see if there is any appreciable play between the spindle and the body - if there is then new bushes will be needed.

Undo the disc retaining screws - these will often be split and opened up to stop them coming loose. Use long nosed pliers to close or break off the ends. Before withdrawing the throttle disc make sure the rebuilt kit includes new discs along with the new shaft - if not mark the old disc so it can be replaced the same way up and the same way round. Remove the disc and the shaft from the carburettor body.

The body will need to be bored out the accept the new bushes - usually these are 9.5 mm. diameter. This is best achieved in a lathe as it is almost impossible to keep the boring concentric and in line any other way. The depth of the bore should match the depth of the new bearing - do not break through to the inner face. If you are not happy about tackling this process give the job to a competent machine shop rather than risk damaging the carburettor bodies.

With the new bearings in place fit the new shaft and manoeuvre the disc into place until it is a snug fit in the body with the throttle closed. Fit the new screws and tighten fully - opening up the split ends to prevent them loosening. Secure the operating levers and spring ensuring that there is a 0.015in. clearance between the lever and the carburettor body. This throttle operating lever is fixed to the shaft by a taper pin. With the throttle held closed the hole for the pin is drilled in the shaft maintaining the clearance mentioned above and a clearance of 0.125in. between the lever and the stop on the carburettor body.

The main jet should be replaced along with the packing and the cork seal in the jet locking nut. Soaking the cork seal in thin oil for some time before fitting helps soften it and likewise the gland packing is best dipped in oil before fitting. Assemble the jet bearings but do not tighten fully the locking nut at this stage. Fit the new needle to the piston, ensuring that the shoulder is flush with the face of the piston, and tighten the securing screw. Fit the piston spring and suction chamber to the carburettor body, ensuring the alignment marks are in the correct position. Do not fit the damper.

The jet must be centred correctly. To do this remove the jet and take off the adjusting nut spring. Replace the nut and the jet and screw the nut up as far as possible. Push the jet up as far as it will go and slacken the jet securing nut - if tightened. Push the piston down, with a rod, lightly against the jet and tighten the securing nut. Remove the jet, replace the spring and nut and replace the jet, screw the adjusting nut fully up. When the piston is raised and dropped it should fall onto the bridge of the carburettor body with a click and feel quite free. If it does not fall freely then the jet is still not correctly centred and the process must be repeated.

The float chamber must now be assembled and the fuel level set. With the standard needle valve the fork must be adjusted so that with a 7/16in. diameter bar (a drill bit will suffice) between the forked lever and the float chamber lid the needle valve is just closed. If fitting 'Gros Jet' valves follow the instructions with them.

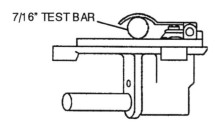

7/16" TEST BAR

The carburettor can then be fully assembled and attached to the inlet manifold. Take care to assemble the linkages correctly and to see that the float bowls are set as far from the heat of the exhaust manifold as possible on the pushrod cars to minimise heat transfer.

SETTING UP THE CARBURETTORS

There is no mystery about setting up S.U. carburettors and no special equipment is needed but one of the simple balancing devices that measures air flow to each carburettor, such as that made by Gunsons, will help, although a piece of pipe was the only thing I used for many years!

The workshop manual and the driver's handbook give good instructions which I need not repeat here. However, I have found it easiest to set up the carburettors as best I can BEFORE starting the engine. To do this make sure that the choke control operates both jets together and pulls them down fully. Screw both jets fully up and then down about two full turns of the adjusting nut. Check that the throttle is operating both throttles simultaneously and that the choke fast idle controls are harmonised and are clear of the throttle stops when the choke is pushed fully off. Remember to top up the piston

dampers with the correct oil. This oil is now available specially packed in small dispensers, but any light oil, about SAE 20, will do temporarily if the correct type is not to hand.

When adjusting the mixture remember that the instructions given in the manual about lifting the piston means that it should only be lifted about 1/32in. (0.8mm) using either the lifting pin or a fine bladed screwdriver - lifting the piston too far is useless when testing the mixture. If the mixture is rich when the piston is lifted the engine speed increases a lot. If the engine speeds up initially and then settled back down to about the same as previously the mixture is correct. If the engine speed decreases then the mixture is too weak and the adjusting nut needs turning downwards.

It is easier to do this with the air cleaners removed but if using the original filters the mixture richens slightly when they are replaced and the carburettors may need weakening a flat or two.

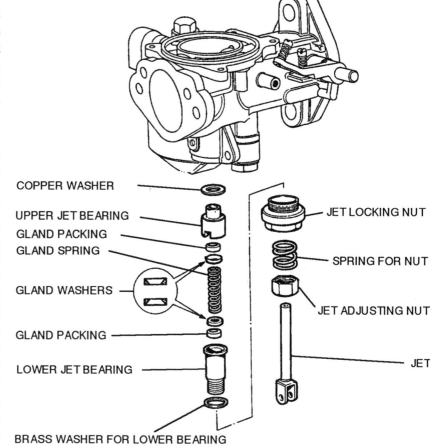

COPPER WASHER

UPPER JET BEARING
GLAND PACKING
GLAND SPRING

GLAND WASHERS

GLAND PACKING

LOWER JET BEARING

JET LOCKING NUT

SPRING FOR NUT

JET ADJUSTING NUT

JET

BRASS WASHER FOR LOWER BEARING

One of the good things about restoring a popular car is the wide choice of spares available. It is possible to buy brand new carburettors off the shelf and ready to fit. However, this is expensive and with a little time and care most old units can be rebuilt at home to perform - and look - as good as these new units.

The correct assembly for the air cleaners of the standard car. The finish is satin black and there are felt pads either side of the filter. There is a cutout in each of the pads but this is only needed on one pad to clear the breather pipe.

BRAKES

There is no more important part of any car than the braking system. Anyone rebuilding an MGA must be certain they are competent to handle the work involved and if they are in any doubt then the job must be entrusted to a professional or be carefully checked by one before the car is used - if the brakes fail there may be no second chance.

There is a popular belief now that the all drum system on the 1500 is no good and the brakes poor. In fact the system is very good and for a car having only infrequent use has some advantages over the disc brakes which can tend to rust discs badly if left unused for periods in

a damp atmosphere. Of course, the disc brakes don't fade so easily if used hard but the drums are quite adequate so long as their limitations are realised. The initial bite of drum brakes make their use in normal day to day driving perfectly acceptable.

The root of most complaints of bad brakes seems to be centred around some poor lining materials that are around and of drums now past their best. Good brake lining materials are available, as well as competition specification linings. However, do not fit the latter unless it is intended to use the brakes very hard as pedal effort is much increased. New brake drums are available and should be used to replace any drums that are badly scored or have been skimmed over size. Always check shoes to drums to make sure there is a good contact. Skimmed drums will reduce the contact patch on the shoes and thus the efficiency of the brakes.

Parts for the drum braked cars are all available at the time of writing as are those for both the disc brakes of the 1600 and the all-disc Twin Cam and de-luxe. However, 1600 brake callipers are in short supply but old units can be re-sleeved and some suppliers are sourcing replacement items. Luckily, with the exception of the master cylinders, all the parts for the all-disc system have been kept in production because of their similarity to the Jaguar Mk II.

On any car being rebuilt it is probably best to strip and examine the whole of the braking system. If the car has been standing for any time, unless silicon brake fluid was used, the cylinders will have corroded and pistons seized. Completely stripping the system will enable it to be refilled with silicon fluid to avoid future problems.

There have been stories in the club magazines of trouble with brake systems where silicon fluid has been used but I have not experienced any myself. The advantages where a car has infrequent use are many, but I am not sure I would use it on a competition car without seeking advice.

REBUILDING THE BRAKING SYSTEM

The pipework was originally plated steel and this available from motor factors but is less easily formed and bent than the copper pipes usually supplied by specialists as kits. A good alternative to copper is cupro-nickle pipe which looks closer in colour to the original steel but is easier to work and is corrosion resistant. This pipe is readily available from motor parts suppliers in 25ft. lengths and is not much more expensive than copper. Provided care is taken the various D.I.Y. pipe flaring tools available are adequate to form the flares on the ends of the pipes and all the fittings needed can be easily purchased. I saved the cost of the tool on the first set of pipes I made up.

As I have said previously, do not attempt to work on the brakes unless you are happy that you have the necessary knowledge and skills. Remember that the fittings need to be in place on the pipe before the ends are flared and that there are two types of flares dependent on which

fitting is used. The instructions for making these flares are included with the tool. The single flare is used usually where a male fitting is screwed into a union and the double flare where a female fitting is fastened over the end of a flexible brake pipe, for example. An examination of the old pipes will indicate what type of flare is required. These old pipes are also useful to determine the length of the replacement pipework. Making these up yourself means they are the correct length - many kits have pipes that are too long.

Both when gripping the pipes in the flaring tool, and when screwing it into the union, take care not to crush or twist it. When making tight bends with steel pipe use a small pipe bending tool such as that made by Sykes-Pickavant (Tool reference number 025600 is ideal). Make sure the pipe runs are neat and are clipped to the chassis and bulkhead as they were originally.

If the master cylinder and the wheel cylinders are to be rebuilt then the cylinder bores must be perfect. It is not good enough to clean off rust with emery paper and expect the seals to hold. The surface must be carefully prepared and if there is any appreciable rusting they will have to be either replaced or re-sleeved by a competent specialist.

A recurring problem with some rebuilt MGAs centres around the master cylinder. The symptom is brakes binding on after they have been used once or twice and for this to get progressively worse. The temptation is to start messing about with the wheel cylinders in the hope of finding a cure but usually this is not the problem.

To check if the fault is in the master cylinder, open one of the bleed nipples on a wheel cylinder when the brakes are seizing. If a spurt of fluid emerges and the brakes free off then the problem is in the master cylinder. There is a bleed hole in the cylinder which is covered when brakes are applied but should be open when the pedal is released to allow any excess fluid to return to the reservoir. If this fluid cannot return, especially as it heats up in use, the brakes will not free off. Some of the seals in repair kits seem to be a bit too large and cover the bleed hole - replacement of the seals is the only cure. However, the same symptoms occur if the free movement on the brake pedal is not maintained and the piston is not allowed to return to the off position.

When fitting the back plates, especially on those of the

1500 front brakes, make sure they are the right way round. If the front plates are wrongly mounted then the system is converted from twin leading shoes to twin trailing shoes and very poor braking results!

When fitting the disc brake callipers make certain the hose support brackets are in place and that the hose is correctly fixed. The brackets are to ensure that the hose does not foul the wheel on full lock. Once everything is assembled, put a wheel on the stub axle and look at it with the wheels on full lock to see the hose stays clear and that it is not pulled too tightly.

If using silicon fluid then the braking system can be filled and bled as soon as it is installed - it is easy with the body off the chassis. If all the components are new, and no trace of the old fluid remains, do not refill with conventional fluid until the car is ready for use, especially if this may be some time ahead.

The handbrake system is easily rebuilt on pushrod cars and, provided all wear in clevis pins, etc. is removed, will work well. At the time of writing complete new handbrake levers and mechanisms are shortly to be available. On the all-disc braked cars the handbrake needs careful assembly and adjustment to provide enough braking power to pass the M.O.T.; this is a common problem on cars with disc rear brakes.

When fitting new discs it is essential to follow the workshop manual instructions about checking the run-out with a dial gauge. If, after trying all the four available positions for the disc, and making sure the mating surfaces are clean and free of rust or debris, the readings are still not within tolerance then the disc is warped. Return new items to the suppliers or replace old ones with new.

After a newly rebuilt car has done a few miles remember to re-adjust the brakes and top up the fluid reservoir.

CHAPTER SEVEN

ELECTRICAL EQUIPMENT

The electrical equipment fitted to MGA's was supplied by Lucas and in dealing with this I will give the part numbers, where I have them, to help when looking for parts at autojumbles. These numbers often have a suffix, i.e. 12345A, but this can for most purposes be ignored when searching.

The instruments were all supplied by Smiths but the faces carried the Jaeger name. Where the instruments need refurbishment this should be put in hand early on in the restoration for reasons I will cover later.

THE DASHBOARD AND INSTRUMENTS.

It is important to note that the basic pressing for the dashboard panel for the coupe differs from that fitted to the open cars. This is a point worth remembering if converting a LHD coupe to RHD, as replacement coupe dashboards are not available. On the 1500 and 1600 the dashboard was painted to match the bodywork, except if this was finished in black when the dashboard was usually painted to tone with the upholstery. On the Twin Cam, all coupes and 1600 Mk II's the dashboard was covered with rexine to match the upholstery and there was a chrome finishing strip on the lower edge.

Now to the instruments themselves. If the car has been driven then the state of these will have become apparent. In a lot of cases the water temperature gauge capillary tube will have been damaged and will need replacing.

Often it will be found that speedometers have been replaced with similar, but perhaps wrongly geared, instruments from, for example, an MGB. The reference number on the dial will help to identify any wrong instruments and a list of the types fitted to MGA's is given on the next page.

If it is decided that the instruments need rebuilding then do not try to take them apart yourself. One of the leading instrument restorers, John Marks of Vintage Restorations, says that this is one of the major causes of difficulties for them as many enthusiasts cause damage trying to dismantle the instruments themselves. The delicate lugs on the rims are bent and broken, cases split and pointers damaged. Almost anything can be replaced or repaired but will add to the cost of renovating the instrument.

The instrument should be taken to the restorer as early as possible in the rebuild. He may take quite a long time to complete the job, especially if any parts of the instruments are missing or broken, and it is very frustrating to he held up at the end waiting for the instruments to be finished. When you give, or send, the instruments for restoration ask for a written receipt and a price quotation and also indicate when they are needed back. This will assist with budgeting to meet the cost and also help the restorer to return them in time.

Something to consider before sending the speedometer

LIST OF SMITHS CODE NUMBERS ON INSTRUMENTS

From Smiths parts lists:-

Speedometers (0-120 mph)

Early 1500	4.3:1	SN6104/02 (miles per hour)
		SN6104/03 (kilometres per hour)
Optional	4.55:1	SN6104/01 (kilometres per hour)

from chassis 14090

1500/1600/Twin Cam	4.3:1	SN6104/06 (Miles per hour)
		SN6104/07 (kilometres per hour)
	from Sept. 1958	SN6161/06 (miles per hour)
		SN6161/07 (kilometres per hour)
	optional 4.55:1	SN6104/09 (miles per hour)
		SN6104/10 (kilometres per hour)
	from Sept. 1958	SN6161/17 (miles per hour)
		SN6161/18 (kilometres per hour)

| Optional 4.875 (Twin Cam) | SN6161/25 (miles per hour) |
| | SN6161/26 (kilometres per hour) |

The change in September 1958 was to the internal ratios. The turns per mile for the 4.3:1 ratio changed from 1450 to 1440 and for the 4.55:1 from 1550 to 1536.

| 1600 Mk II 4.1:1 | SN6161/12 (miles per hour) |
| | SN6161/33 (kilometres per hour) |

Rev. counters

Early 1500	51-112-102-00
1500 from chassis 14090/1600 (0-7,000 rpm)	RN2350/01
Twin Cam (0-7,500 rpm)	RN2300/02
1600 Mk II (0-7,000 rpm)	RN2350/01

Fuel Gauge.

| Early 1500 | FG 2530/25 |
| 1500 from chassis 14090/1600/Twin Cam/1600 Mk II | FG2530/05 |

Fuel tank sender unit (all models) FT 5300/20
(Models fitted with the large competition fuel tank used FG2530/05 gauge and FT5346/43 sender unit.)

Oil Pressure/Water Temperature Dual Gauge.

Early 1500	GD 1501/00
1500 from chassis 14090/1600/Twin Cam/ 1600 Mk II	
	GD1501/04 (Fahrenheit)GD1501/04 (Centigrade)

to the restorer is the final drive ratio fitted to the car and the tyre choice. If the specification has been changed from standard the restorer will need to be told to modify the speedometer gearing accordingly. He will need to know the number of turns the speedometer cable makes per mile of road covered.

If the car is mobile then there is a simple method of calculating this. Disconnect the cable from the speedometer and make a small card pointer to fit on the inner cable. With the tyres at the correct pressure, measure the radius from the centre of the rear hub to the ground. Make a chalk mark on the rear tyre and push the car along until the wheel has revolved exactly six

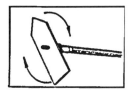

A small card pointer is attached to the inner cable of the speedometer drive.

times, counting the number of turns the shaft makes. The number of turns per mile is calculated by multiplying the number of turns of the shaft by 1680 and dividing the result by the radius in inches. An example:- if the shaft turns 9.2 times multiply this by 1680 and divide by the radius (in this case 12.5 ins.) to work out the T.P.M., in this example 1236.

The design of the face of the instruments was changed from 1500 chassis number 14090 with the large markings at 20 mph and 1000 rpm increments replaced by smaller lettering but marked every 10 mph and 500 rpm. The speedometer for the Twin Cam was the same as the pushrod cars, only being changed with differing axle ratios as was the case also with the standard engined cars. The Twin Cam rev. counter, however, was different with the red section starting at 7000 rpm rather than 6000 rpm. Peter wood, the Twin Cam specialist, has produced a supply of dials for these instruments.

The cockpit of an early 1500 showing the style of instruments used up to chassis number 14089.

SWITCHES, ETC.

Ignition key switch S45 part number 31449F.

Flashing indicators switch (self-cancelling) TPS1 (31250H)

Flashing indicators warning light WL13 green lens (38132A)

Panel light switch - with rheostat CHR1 or 3R (78311A or 78346E, knob marked 'P' 768945)

Fog lamp switch - PS7 (31515A, knob marked 'F' 312866)

Light switch - pull type PPG1 (31251D, knob marked 'L' 316154)

Horn push HP19 (76205D)

Optional headlamp flasher switch 235A (31898A)

Optional headlamp flasher relay DB10 (33117D) or SB40 (33135)

Wiper switch - PS7 (31515A, knob marked 'W' 312865)

Stop lamp switch in brake line HL2 (31082H)

Map light 534 (53763A, cover 574825, glass 573915)

Map light switch - DS7 (31515A, knob without marking 316102)

Many of the modern replacement switches have wrongly shaped fixing nuts - correct items are now available from some suppliers (Anglo Parts for example).

Batteries originally Lucas SG9E.

Dynamo

1500 early with windows C39 PV-2 (22258DE, later, without windows, 22258EF)

1600 C40 or C40-1 (22704A/D or 22700)

Twin Cam C39 PV2 with different pulley (22295)

Dynamos are simple pieces of equipment that give very little trouble in service. The brushes and bearings should be checked and replaced if necessary. Exchange, rebuilt units are available if the original is badly worn. The front bearing is a ball race and replacements are available from specialists or from any bearing supplier. Originally these were lubricated when the dynamo was assembled and then left as no provision for oiling in service exists. If replacing this bearing consider using one of the modern sealed-for-life type which can be obtained in the exact size. When removing the old bearing take care not to damage the end plate. On most dynamos there is a bearing plate riveted to the end plate with three rivets that will have to be drilled out. Take care to note the number and positions of the washers.

The plain bearing at the rear end of the dynamo is provided with lubrication and is usually not very worn. If replacing, it must be pressed from the end cover using a shouldered mandrel - easily turned up from steel bar in a lathe. The new oilite bearing must be soaked in oil for as long as possible before inserting.

To check the dynamo circuits with the dynamo in the car disconnect the two leads from the dynamo and connect a voltmeter between the larger terminal and a good earth. At 1500 rpm the voltmeter should read between 1.5 and 3 volts. Then with the voltmeter still connected as above connect an ammeter between the two terminals of the dynamo. Increase the engine speed

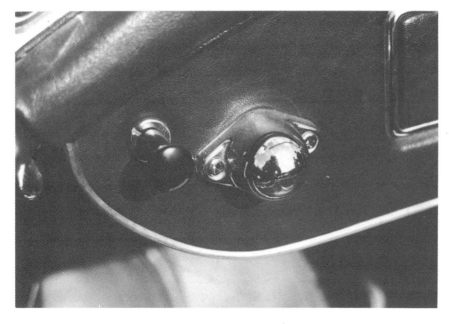

The neat map reading light which is operated by the pull switch along-side it. The knob does not have any lettering on it.

until the voltmeter reads 12 volts. The ammeter should then read approximately 2 amp. Any higher reading suggests the field resistance in the dynamo is low and a rebuild by an auto electrician or a replacement is called for. The connectors changed to lucar type from chassis 74489.

Dynamos were painted engine colour all over - including the end plates.

Control Box
RB106-2 (37182H/J, later 37183M)
From chassis 74489 the control box had Lucar connectors instead of the original screw type.

Control boxes will work happily for years without attention but unfortunately they are often tampered with by the unknowledgeable in an attempt to cure faults that probably have their origin elsewhere. The method of checking, for the early type, that the cut out is adjusted correctly is given in the workshop manual but basically consists of connecting a voltmeter between terminal D and E and checking that the contacts close when the engine speed rises. The correct reading is 12.7 to 13.3 volts and there is an adjustable screw provided to change the setting. Adjustments for later type are also given. The points can be cleaned CAREFULLY with fine emery paper.

As I said previously, don't mess around with the settings unless absolutely necessary because the likelihood is that they are probably right anyway - provided someone else hasn't had a go at them.

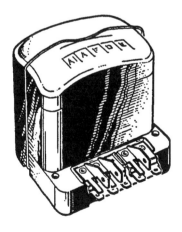

The control box used from chassis 74489 had Lucar connectors.

Modern replacement boxes bearing the Lucas name are now made in the Far East and not in Birmingham. They look similar, and seem to work, but the bobbins are much smaller than the original items.

Starter Motor
M35G-1 (25022) changing on the late 1600 Mk II to M35G (25079B/D)
Starters usually need little more than a clean and checkover. Brushes and bearings may need attention on a high mileage car and wear in the Bendix can occur. Parts are available but so are exchange units. In almost all cases though the starter will probably only need the gears cleaned and freed off and lightly oiled for it to work well for many miles. Starters were painted in engine colour.

A word of warning here. If the starter only turns over very slowly, or hardly at all, when you first try to start the car after a rebuild, check that the earth strap between the engine and chassis is in place and making good contact. It is all too easy to forget this and the earth provided through the loom is insufficient for the starter load and the loom will burn out.

Starter switch under bonnet (hood) ST19-2 (76701A, coupling 764428, boot 860556)
Often parts suppliers will offer a later style rubber boot as fitted to MGB's but the correct, earlier style is now available from some of them and looks much better.

Coil
All cars were fitted with the HA12 coil (45054K) but the mounting point changed with the 1500 cars having the coil on the top of the dynamo and the 1600's on a

COIL MOUNTING

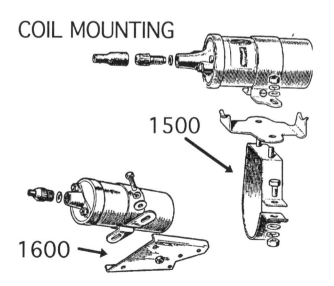

1500

1600

bracket on the right-hand engine mounting. On the Twin Cam the coil was mounted on the inner wing. On some de-luxe models, which used up surplus Twin Cam bodies, the coil was mounted on the top of the dynamo - as on the 1500.

Coils cannot be repaired and any damage or corrosion on the case can allow moisture to enter, causing damage. If there is any doubt then replace - remembering to connect the wires to the terminals the correct way round.

Fusebox SF6 (033239) was fitted to all cars.

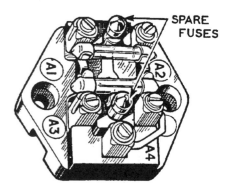

The twin batteries. Fitting these is certainly a lot easier with the body removed!

Coil mounting on the 1500 and some de luxe models where the Twin Cam chassis was used.

Wiper Motor

DA48 (RHD) DA49 (LHD) later quoted as DR2 on all cars (part number 75297)

Usually these benefit from a careful clean. If completely stripped, pitted aluminium components can be carefully bead blasted to restore a fine, matt surface. A fine spray of clear lacquer will keep this finish. Replacement wheelboxes, rack and rack covers are available as are the chrome plated spindles. The switch that adjusts the parking position will need to be moved on cars converted from left to right hand drive. The wipers always parked on the driver's side. The wiper arms differed for RHD (745022) and LHD (745083) but both are available from parts suppliers.

Horn

The standard horn was a windtone WT618L (69046F) with the option of an additional high note WT618H (69047F).

Problems with the horn are more usually due to the mounting bolts being loose or to faulty wiring. If after checking these points the horn still does not work, try removing the cover and slackening the lock nut. Rotate the adjusting nut until the horn sounds and then back it off until the contacts just separate (and the horn stops). Turn the nut in the opposite direction a quarter turn and tighten the lock nut. Test the horn and adjust further if necessary.

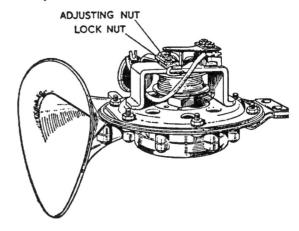

ADJUSTING THE HORN

The MGA 1600 cockpit. When this photograph was taken in 1976 I owned the car and the mileage was only 24,220. The instruments are the type used on all MGAs after chassis 14090.

Lights

Headlamps. The headlamps were F700 units but for overseas markets various different versions of the units were fitted. At first the USA had US built sealed beam units and later on Lucas sealed beam units.

Sidelamps. (*First series Twin Cam as 1500, second series as 1600*)
Front 1500 539 (52236A)
         1600 632 (52425D)
         LHD USA, etc. all white lamp 630 (52430E)
Rear 1500 549 (53330D)
         1600 549 (53330D) but also had separate
         flashers 594 (52337B amber and 53600E red).
1600 Mk II 647 (LH 53964A, RH 53965A and
         North America LH 53966A and RH 53967A)

1600 rear lights.

1500 rear lights.

1600 and 1600 Mk II front side lights.

1500 front side lights.

1600 Mk II rear lights.

Number plate lamp 467 (53093) changed to two bulb type from 1600, chassis 88844, 467-2 (53836F). For Switzerland a 469 unit was fitted (53905A)

Fog lamp (optional extra) SFT 576 (55128E). If two lamps fitted in USA relay SB40 (33223) was used.

Flasher Unit FL5 or FL3

Flasher Relay (1500 and first series Twin Cam only) DB10 (33117D).

Distributor.

The 1500 (except first few cars) and 1600 had a DM2P4 distributor (part number 40510) and the 1600 Mk II a DM2P4 distributor (part number 40761)

The Twin Cam initially had the same unit but this was replaced by a 23D4 distributor without a vacuum advance and this is a recommended fitting for the earlier models. The standard distributor had 22-26 degrees of auto advance with the vacuum disconnected and the replacement 24-28 degrees but no vacuum advance. In all cases the cap is part number 42290S, the rotor 400051, the contacts 423153 and the condenser 423871. The plug caps were Lucas right angled type, number 78106.

Although a simple device more poor running can be attributed to a worn or incorrect distributor that to any other component, save perhaps the carburettors. The trouble is that it is not possible to see all the faults on a distributor just by examining it. If at any time the auto advance weights or springs have been tampered with, or are just plain worn out, then the advance curve will no longer match the original specification. For this reason suspect any unit until it is proved correct. Using a stroboscopic light a rough check on the advance can be made. The standard distributor should give 22-26 degrees of advance, with the vacuum disconnected, at higher engine speeds. However, to have the distributor advance curve checked accurately requires more sophisticated equipment.

If the distributor is worn, with noticeable play in the shaft, then the bearings will need replacing. These bearings are available but will need careful reaming in line once fitted. A number of companies will supply either reconditioned or new distributors set up to the MGA specification, which may be a good investment in view of the importance of this component for good performance.

One specialist advertises that the rebuild consists of stripping and removing old bushes, testing all components for wear, bead blasting the body and replacing other components. He fits new bushes and assembles the distributor with new cap, vacuum unit, condenser and contacts. The complete assembly is then checked against the original manufacturer's advance curve on a diagnostic test machine. At the time of writing the cost for this was £85.

A part often overlooked when assembling the front side lights is the plastic washer. This washer fits between the lens and the foam seal to allow the lens to turn, when removing or fitting, without twisting the foam seal. The 1500 parts seen here also include the rear seal that fits between the base and the car bodywork. In addition a rubber boot fits over the wiring, inside the wing.

Heater

The heater was always an optional extra on MGA's and quite a number of cars, especially those delivered to overseas markets, were not fitted with them. Where neither the heater nor a fresh air unit was installed the hole in the scuttle was covered with a pressed steel blanking plate painted black. The fresh air unit was really just the heater unit without any of the water connections or heater matrix and with the casing modified accordingly.

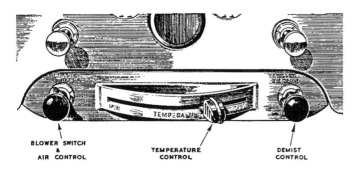

BLOWER SWITCH & AIR CONTROL   TEMPERATURE CONTROL   DEMIST CONTROL

The controls for the heater changed early in the life of the 1500 but unfortunately the parts books record the change but not the change point. On the early cars (above) the blower motor was switched on by turning the air control knob; whereas on the later models (below) the temperature selector knob was pulled to operate the motor.

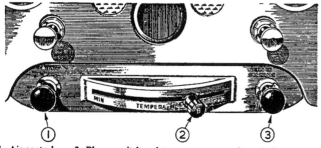

1. Air control.   2. Blower switch and temperature control.   3. Demist control

There were two types of heater fitted to MGA's. Type FHR 2453/01 for all pushrod cars and FHR 2457/01 for the Twin Cam. Both types used the same motor, FHM 5332 and looked similar, but the casing was entirely different and a pushrod unit cannot be made to fit a Twin Cam. Until recently this posed problems for anyone wanting to install a heater in a car not previously equipped with one but luckily all the parts and, indeed, complete heater units are again available. These are constructed of parts made largely on the original tooling and in some cases by the original manufacturers.

There are some internal changes on these new units with both the impeller fan and the heater matrix being replaced by more recent versions offering greater efficiency. As these modifications are not seen from the outside then they should not worry even the most ardent purist.

Restoring an Old Unit

With all the parts of the heater now back in production it has become easier to restore old units. Stripping a heater down is easy as the parts are, in the main, just clipped together with plated clips and these can either be replated or replaced with new clips. The metal casing can be stripped of paint and any areas of light rusting treated with a proprietary rust preventative. Alternatively these parts could be lightly bead blasted. After careful preparation the parts can then be sprayed or powder coated. Originally they were finished in a satin finish - i.e. not very shiny - black paint. Reproductions of the makers stickers are available although these are not always exactly the same as those fitted originally as these were changed slightly during the production run of the MGA.

The heater motors are generally very reliable and give little trouble but if one does fail new units are available. The motor has specially shaped rubber bushes to isolate it from the mounting bracket to avoid undue noise being transmitted into the cockpit. New bushes are available if needed.

The heater matrix can be blocked with scale and is easily damaged when handled. As any leaks will result in the contents of the cooling system ending up in the cockpit it is obviously important to check it before installation. When replacing it in the heater box note the position of the various pieces of felt and also sealing grommets around the water inlet and outlet pipes.

The vent flaps inside the car are often very rusty, especially if the heater has been leaking. These can usually be bead blasted and repainted, or new units (which are made to the original pattern and still in use on some commercial vehicles) could be fitted. When fitting the pipes to the demisters note that there are adapting collars to link the pipes to the outlet vents by the windscreen. These are often omitted with the result that the pipes drop off!

As the heater does not drain completely always use anti-freeze or corrosion inhibitor in the cooling system.

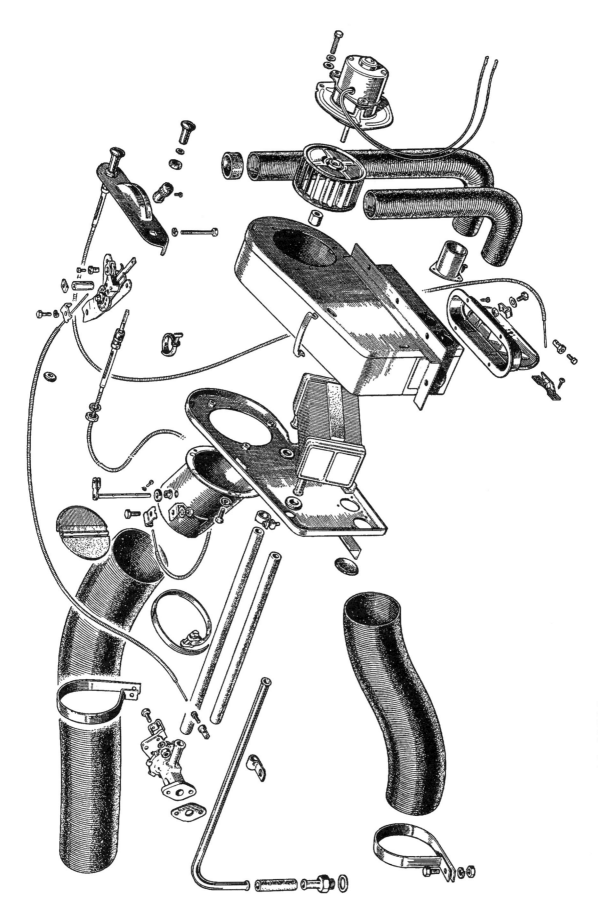

The components of the MGA heater

A new heater matrix which has a higher output than the original unit but is a direct replacement. The matrix is sealed round the edges with felt strips within the heater box to force all the air through the matrix. A contact adhesive is used to fasten the felt in place - do not use too much.

The original type pressed steel impeller alongside a modern plastic replacement. The new fan is more efficient and the light yellow colour is hidden when the heater is fully assembled.

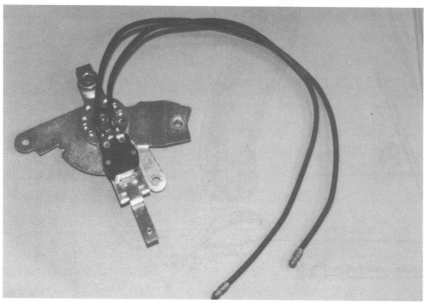

A new blower switch and temerature control. The early type of control is not availabe but this type could probably be modified to fit an early car.

The fuel pump and mounting on a pushrod car. The pump is bolted to a bracket which is then bolted to the chassis. This bracket is isolated by rubber pads which act to reduce the amount of vibration reaching the pump. The mounting system is identical to that used on the T-types.

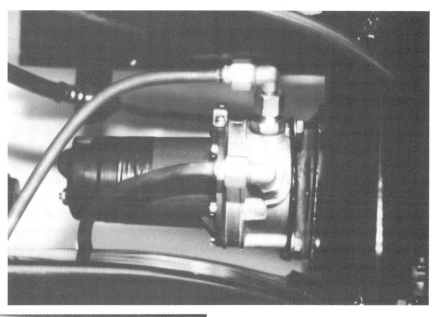

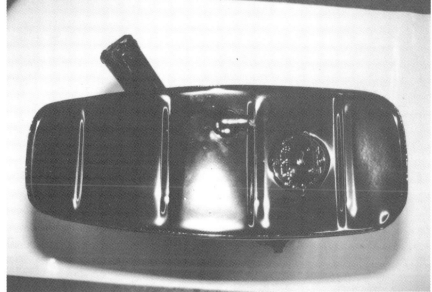

The fuel tank is vulnerable but out of sight and it pays, therefore, to protect it well. Even a brand new tank would benefit from being stripped and powder coated as this tank has been. The fuel gauge sender unit is mounted in the end of the tank and care must be taken to obtain a fuel tight seal when it is installed - working on it later, when the car is finished, is not so easy. The tank support straps can also be powder coated.

Just a reminder to fit the earth strap! Make sure enough paint is cleaned off the components to obtain a good electrical contact.

When filling the cooling system initially check that the heater is fully filled by loosening the outlet pipe from the heater box to the head once the engine has been run and the water heated. Make sure that it has reached this point but take care not to scald yourself!

FUEL PUMP

The fuel pump fitted to all MGAs was an S.U. high pressure pump. The pushrod cars had an AUA 54 (later AUA 154) with the Twin Cam having the higher capacity LCS type AUA 73. Replacements pumps to both specifications are available at the time of writing. Current reference numbers AZX 1332 for pushrod cars and AZX 1319 for the Twin Cam.

Used regularly the fuel pump is reliable but with infrequent use the points can corrode giving rise to the need to give the thing a 'bash' to make it start ticking again! Cleaning and resetting the points as described in the manual usually helps. Replacement parts, including diaphragm and spindle assemblies are available. Before fitting any new pump it is advisable to take the end cap off and wipe the points with a degreasing agent to remove any protective film from them.

The fuel lines from the tank to the pump and from the pump to the bulkhead were originally plated steel. Replacement parts are usually copper but to maintain originality consider having steel pipes made - most larger garages, especially those servicing commercial vehicles, will have supplies of the pipe in either steel or cupro-nickle which looks closer in colour than copper. Always replace the flexible pipes to the carburettors as the inner rubber pipe perishes.

CHAPTER EIGHT

PAINTWORK

Rightly or wrongly the casual observer will usually judge a car primarily by the standard of the paintwork. The paintwork is, of course, the first thing seen when looking at a car and, no matter how well the restoration of the other components has been done, if the paintwork is not good the whole restoration will be written off by them as second rate. As well as considering the standard of paint finish, it is also important to try to achieve the right look for a car that is being restored to original condition. Although one may not always wish to repaint the car the same colour it originally left the factory and, indeed, may wish to use a colour never used by M.G. on any MGA, any colour used should suit the car and be 'in period'. Some of the modern 'metallic' and 'flake' finishes may look good on more recent vehicles but are out of place on the MGA. When working on a car with such a beautifully designed body it is a pity to spoil it with an inappropriate paint finish.

If choosing a different standard paint colour remember that the trim colours were only available with certain body colours. Old English White cars, for example, did not have green or tan trim. Some cars left the factory in primer and as kits for assembly overseas and these were sometimes finished in colours never listed in factory publications. However, for what it is worth, listed below are all the standard colours and variations gleaned from the colour charts, sales brochures and parts lists available.

1500 (roadster)
Black (BK1, ICI 2007) with Red or Green trim. Ice Blue or black hood and tonneau cover.
Orient Red (RD3, ICI 2935) with Red or Black trim and Black hood and tonneau cover.
Old English White (WT3, ICI 2379) Red trim or Black trim/White piping. Black hood and tonneau cover.
Glacier Blue (BU4, ICI 2984) with Grey trim or Black trim/Grey piping. Ice Blue or Black hood and tonneau.
Tyrolite Green (GN7, ICI 2985) used up to roadster number 48999 with Grey trim or Black trim/Green piping and Ice Blue or Black hood and tonneau cover.
Ash Green (GN2, ICI 3221) from roadster 49000 with Grey trim or Black trim/Green piping and Ice Blue or Black hood and tonneau cover.

1500 (coupe)
Black (BK1, ICI 2007) with Red or Green trim and Black dashboard.
Orient Red (RD3, ICI 2935) with Red or Black trim and red dashboard.
Old English White (WT3 ICI 2379) with Red trim or Black trim/White piping and White dashboard.
Island Green (GN6, ICI 5019) used up to coupe number 48979 with Grey trim or Black trim/Green piping and green dashboard.
Ash Green (GN2, ICI 3221) from coupe 48980 with Grey trim or Black trim/Green piping and green dashboard.
Mineral Blue (BU9, ICI 3130) with Grey trim and

dashboard or Black trim/Blue piping and Blue dashboard.

1600 and 1600 Mk II (roadster)

Black (BK1, ICI 2007) with Beige or Red trim and dashboard either painted to match trim (1600) or covered (Twin Cam and Mk II) to match trim. Hood and tonneau cover Grey.

Chariot Red (RD16, ICI 3344) with Red or Beige trim or Black trim/Red piping and dashboard painted Red (1600) or covered (Twin Cam and Mk II) to match trim. Hood and tonneau cover Beige with Red or Beige trim and Grey with Black trim.

Iris Blue (BU12, ICI 3243) with Black trim/Blue piping and dashboard painted Iris Blue (1600) or covered (Twin Cam and Mk II) in Black. Hood and tonneau cover Light Blue.

Alamo Beige (BG9, ICI 3343) with Red trim and dashboard painted Alamo Beige (1600) or covered (Twin Cam and Mk II) in Red. Hood and tonneau cover Beige.

Dove Grey (GR26, ICI 3346) with Red trim and dashboard painted Grey (1600) or covered (Twin Cam and Mk II) in Red. Hood and tonneau cover Grey.

Old English White (WT3, ICI 2379) with Red trim or Black trim/White piping and dashboard painted White (1600) or covered (Twin Cam and Mk II) to match trim. Hood and tonneau cover Grey.

1600 and 1600 Mk II (coupe)

Black (BK1, ICI 2007) with Beige or Red trim.

Chariot Red (RD16, ICI 3344) with Red or Beige trim or Black trim/Red piping.

Iris Blue (BU12, ICI 3243) with Black trim/Blue piping.

Alamo Beige (BG9, ICI 3343) with Red trim.

Dove Grey (GR26, ICI 3346) with Red trim.

Old English White (WT3, ICI 2379) with Red trim or Black trim/White piping.

Dashboards covered to match trim.

Twin Cam (roadster and coupe)

The first series cars - up to chassis 2192 colours and trim as 1500.

The second series cars - from chassis 2193 colours and trim as 1600.

NOTE: On 1600 Mk II the scuttle top was covered to reduce reflection in the windscreen. On Black cars the covering was black, on Red cars it was red except with black trim when covering was black, Iris Blue had black covering, Alamo Beige had red, as did Dove Grey, and Old English White had either red or black according to colour of trim.

The parts list shows that the white piping behind the facia trim rail on Old English White coupes was changed to black from chassis 100596.

Now for a word of warning. Armed with the original colour code you might think that it is an easy task to obtain paint to match that originally supplied to M.G. to paint the MGA. However, a look round any group of restored cars at meetings will reveal any number of different shades of Orient Red or Iris Blue! All the owners will be convinced that they have used the correct colour but they all cannot be right. The answer lies in the basic pigments used by the modern paint manufacturers and their relationship to the old paint formulae.

Paint manufacture has changed greatly over the last few years and many of the constituent pigments used, even a short while ago, are no longer permitted under current health and safety legislation. To take account of this the formulae used have been changed and the colours produced are seldom exactly the same as the original. The modern Iris Blue, for example, is slightly brighter in most cases and the Dove Grey a shade darker. Reds have always been difficult to match - even when the cars were new - but my impression is that these, too, are now just a shade different from the 1950s equivalent. Original factory colour charts I have looked at tend to support my impressions, but it is foolish to rely too much on matching from such small samples that may have faded over the years.

So where does that leave the current restorers? The best advice I can give is to either try to match from any surviving original samples of paint, although this has it's own dangers bearing in mind that the sample you will be working from may have faded, or to obtain a small sample of the chosen colour from the suppliers and to try it out before making any final commitment to a large quantity. Of course, if there is a recently restored car around with exactly the shade of paint required the owner will probably be only too happy to supply the name of the manufacturer and the code.

Whichever colour is chosen it is probably best to have all the paint needed mixed at the same time, together some spare for future touching-in as small quantities mixed later will probably be a slightly different shade.

BODY COLOUR	HOOD (TWO-SEATER ONLY)	LEATHER
ORIENT RED (Two-seater and Coupé)	BLACK	RED OR BLACK
OLD ENGLISH WHITE (Two-seater and Coupé)	BLACK	RED OR BLACK
GLACIER BLUE (Two-seater only)	ICE BLUE	GREY OR BLACK
TYROLITE GREEN (Two-seater only)	ICE BLUE	GREY OR BLACK
ISLAND GREEN (Coupé only)	—	GREY OR BLACK
MINERAL BLUE (Coupé only)	—	GREY OR BLACK

BLACK : WITH ICE BLUE OR BLACK HOOD AND RED OR GREEN LEATHER (Two-seater)
BLACK : WITH RED OR GREEN LEATHER (Coupé)

Publication No. H & E 57-78. The earlier colour chart for the 1500.

BODY COLOUR	HOOD (TWO-SEATER ONLY)	LEATHER
ORIENT RED (Two-seater and Coupé)	BLACK	RED OR BLACK
OLD ENGLISH WHITE (Two-seater and Coupé)	BLACK	RED OR BLACK
GLACIER BLUE (Two-seater only)	ICE BLUE	GREY OR BLACK
ASH GREEN (Two-seater and Coupé)	ICE BLUE	GREY OR BLACK
MINERAL BLUE (Coupé only)	—	GREY OR BLACK

BLACK : WITH ICE BLUE OR BLACK HOOD AND RED OR GREEN LEATHER (Two-seater)
BLACK : WITH RED OR GREEN LEATHER (Coupé)

The later 1500 colour chart showing the change to Ash Green. Publication No. H & E 58-39

SERIES MGA 1600 COLOUR FINISHES

BODY COLOURS	LEATHER	HOOD (TWO-SEATER ONLY)
CHARIOT RED (*Two-seater and Coupé*)	RED BEIGE BLACK	BEIGE BEIGE GREY
IRIS BLUE (*Two-seater and Coupé*)	BLACK	BLUE
ALAMO BEIGE (*Two-seater and Coupé*)	RED	BEIGE
DOVE GREY (*Two-seater and Coupé*)	RED	GREY
OLD ENGLISH WHITE (*Two-seater and Coupé*)	RED BLACK	GREY GREY

BLACK: WITH RED OR BEIGE LEATHER, GREY HOOD (Two-seater)

BLACK: WITH RED OR BEIGE LEATHER (Coupé)

THE ABOVE COLOUR FINISHES AND UPHOLSTERY APPLICABLE ALSO TO THE 'MGA' TWIN CAM

For the 1600 and 1600 Mk II the colour range changed. This is publication No. H & E 5941

An original, unrestored MGA 1600 displays the light blue hood and sidescreens (above). The lower photograph shows just how attractive the painted dashboard can be. The car is finished in Glacier Blue with Grey trim.

Having chosen the colour, which type of paint finish are you going to use for your car? Originally the MGA was finished in cellulose with exception of some Iris Blue cars which were painted in synthetic enamel. Nowadays quite a number of cars are finished with modern 'two-pack' paint which is very much harder wearing than the original finishes. The only problem with this type of paint is that it is totally unsuited to home application unless you have the necessary paint booth and air fed breathing equipment. Indeed, many of even the 'ordinary' cellulose paints now contain quite a cocktail of chemicals and great care should be taken not to breathe them in. Some of the thinners in use are especially potent! As well as breathing in vapour there is also a health risk from skin contact with some of these paints and thinners. All in all I feel the time is fast approaching when legislation will stop us spraying at home and I understand that in some countries there is now a difficulty in obtaining materials for non-trade use. As someone who has had a lot of enjoyment over the years painting my own cars I am sorry that things are going this way.

Having had recent experience of assembling a car painted professionally in two-pack I can testify to it's durability, although I feel the final finish does not look exactly the same as the same colour in cellulose. However, if it is decided to paint the car at home then cellulose is probably the best choice. The slower drying enamel is also suitable but the resulting finish cannot be easily polished and it is essential to achieve a good result 'straight from the gun'. However, on chassis components it has the advantage of being more chip resistant, although not as good as two-pack or powder coating.

Unless there is quite a large area available and the sprayer fairly practised at the art, the amateur will probably find it easier to spray an MGA separated into components, i.e. with wings, doors, boot lid, etc. removed. Alternatively if the car is assembled it should be masked off and sprayed in sections to avoid excessive overspray. With plenty of space, light and high pressure equipment the car can be sprayed in one piece but the chances of mistakes over a larger area are that much greater.

This is not the place for a step by step guide to spray painting, but as an amateur in the field I have painted a few cars over the years and will just point out a few things I have learned the hard way.

MATERIALS AND EQUIPMENT

I have spoken about the colour to be used and the difficulty of matching but far more important is the need to use paint from one manufacturers paint system. Mixing different brands of paint or thinners is not to be recommended unless it is known that no harm will result. The bare steel or aluminium will need first an etch primer followed by a primer or primer filler and then the final colour coats.

There are quite a number of fairly inexpensive compressors and spray guns on the market and elaborate equipment is not necessary for a good result. A compressor with a tank capacity of at least 25 litres and a moisture separator will be quite sufficient, both for spraying and also for other workshop use, although a compressor with high output will be needed to drive air tools or where an air fed mask is to be used in addition to the spray gun. I use a low pressure gun which is suitable for spraying cars that can be reduced to, as far as possible, separate components. Where the car is to be sprayed as a unit a high pressure gun, and a compressor able to feed it, is better.

When using solvents health and safety considerations must be paramount. We are learning now of the long term risks to health of inhaling these solvents so, unless an air fed mask is used, the workshop must be very well ventilated and a mask with removable cartridges worn at all times - both when spraying or when there is dust in the air. For this reason I like to spray outside, or with the garage door open, and take the risk of dust or small flies landing on the fresh paint. Incidentally should an insect land, do not try to remove it from the wet paint, it will soon be overcome by the fumes and will do less damage than will be done trying to lift it off. Most small marks left by the legs of a dead fly can be polished out once the paint has dried.

In addition to a good mask and overalls, rubber gloves are necessary to protect from the thinners and to use when rubbing down.

Most of the paint manufacturers issue detailed sheets giving instructions and recommendations on using their products. I.C.I. have a very useful guide that shows the thinning ratios, type of thinners to use in various conditions and rules on handling, including safety precautions. Instructions like these are a great help in selecting the right products to buy. Using the correct thinners assists in achieving a good result, especially when spraying in less than ideal conditions. I find that I need at least three different thinners to cater for both temperature and humidity changes and also for the different materials being sprayed.

Always use a good quality thinners, compatible to the paint system in use. However, cheap 'gun wash' thinners to use to clean out the spray gun, and to wipe off overspray from tools, etc., will save some money.

There are many grades of 'wet and dry' papers available as well as types like 'Frecut' which are designed to be used dry without undue clogging. I usually make do with some 120 grade for initial rubbing down of any filler prior to painting, 600 and 800 grade for the primer/filler and flatting the top coat, and 1000 or 1200 for final finishing.

PREPARATION

I know that this is often said but I will repeat it here:- good preparation is essential if a good finish is to result. You cannot cover up anything with paint as it is not thick enough to conceal even quite small blemishes. The surface must be really smooth before applying any paint. Any areas of pitting, or small dents that cannot be removed by panel beating, must be filled. The traditional 'lead loading' is not all that difficult to do but it does take a bit of practice and the materials are expensive, and cannot be used on aluminium panels. Good results can be obtained from the various two-pack fillers around but watch out for areas that flex, like the boot lid, as some of these fillers can crack. There are some now that have aluminium particles in them instead of chalk but these do tend to be a bit more difficult to rub down and again some crack if flexed.

If using cellulose do not apply any of these fillers over paint. When spraying, the thinners travels through the previous layers of paint and unsightly dips can appear weeks after finishing the job where the thinners has crept under the edge of the filler. It is better to use a cellulose stopper to fill small blemishes that appear when rubbing down at each stage. This may take longer to dry but at least it will be compatible with the paint. However, do not use cellulose stopper too thickly as this may later shrink, spoiling the finish.

With the use of a random orbit sander rubbing down large areas of filler will be a lot easier. Any area of surface rusting will have to be treated with one of the solutions available but make sure there is no residue left that could affect paint adhesion. Thoroughly clean all the metal and filler with a cleaner such as 'Panelwipe' before going on to apply paint. The surface should also be finally wiped with a 'tack' rag to remove any dust.

PAINTING

On both steel and aluminium apply a coat of etching primer before the primer/filler is sprayed. These etching primers are usually supplied in two parts and have to be mixed before spraying. Usually they will not require further thinning but if this is necessary use the grade of thinners recommended. Do not rub down after this.

Some of the primer/fillers are too thick to spray well with a low pressure gun if thinned to the manufacturer's instructions. Try adding a further 10% of thinners if there is any difficulty. Try not to spray the paint on too 'dry'. It should appear wet and glossy on the surface right after spraying. These paints use a fast thinners and if using them on a hot day, especially out of doors with sun on the panels being sprayed, they can dry as soon as they touch the surface. This dry, gritty finish is difficult to rub down without removing a lot of paint, and quite a lot of tiny air bubbles can be trapped in the paint causing problems later. Although you do not want the paint so thin it 'runs', it should have a chance to flow onto the surface before it starts to dry.

Apply quite a few full coats of primer/filler before even thinking about rubbing down. It is a mistake to rub down too often. Priming coats would not need to be rubbed down more than twice if your surface preparation was good. Often only one rubbing down is needed but do not pass on to the final stages until happy with the result. The secret of getting a good surface for the final coats is to use a guide coat on the primer before rubbing down. I find it useful to have a small quantity of primer of a different colour to hand and will mix some of this into the last coat of the primer to change its colour before spraying. This final coat should just be a light one going all over the panel. When rubbing down, any dips or hollows will show up well and it can be seen if any areas are missed. I like to rub down the last coat before painting colour using 'wet and dry' with a small amount of washing up liquid in the water. Remember to use 'Panelwipe' to clean the surface before applying the final colour. Rubbing down is a time consuming and messy business - do not rush it. The primers are not waterproof and will absorb some water, so allow them plenty of time to dry in the sun before applying top coats.

It is a lot more difficult to rub down gloss top coats than primer. For this reason do not be in a hurry to apply paint to any part you are not entirely happy with. The final colour coats will not cover any blemishes, and as paint is expensive, get the primer right before using any. I said earlier that there will be some difficulty in choosing the right colour. If there is any doubt then ask the supplier to mix a small sample to try. One of the major suppliers in the United Kingdom will let you have a sample tenth of a litre bag of the colour chosen. This is quite enough to spray a reasonably large piece of metal. It is better to try out some paint first before committing yourself to 10 litres of the wrong colour!

The finish achieved with the top coats is dependent on the paint flowing onto the panel without either being so wet it runs, or dry enough to leave a dusty, dull and rough surface. As the paint is first applied it will appear a bit rough but, if there is a good combination of consistency and temperature, the paint will flow to a nice, even gloss finish. If spraying outside remember that the sun will warm a panel quite a lot and the top surface of it may be a lot warmer than the more shaded areas. This will cause inconsistent results and perhaps it would be better to spray the final coat under cover if possible. If you do not want to be shut in with the paint fumes try spraying in the garage with the doors open.

As with the primer, spray a good layer of paint before rubbing down. It is possible to get away with just one rubbing down session before the final coats. Use 800 grade for this, unless the paint is very rough, and use some soap to help wet the surface. After rubbing down the paint should have an even, matt appearance.

If there are a lot of pin holes then the paint has probably been sprayed too thick or with too fast a thinners for the conditions, or even with the gun held too close to the work. As I mentioned, the choice of thinners is important. In high temperatures, or high humidity, use a slow, anti-bloom thinners. I tend to use this also for all final coats as it gives better results.

When satisfied that there is a good surface apply the final coats. These should be applied in one go, making sure that each pass of the gun overlaps the previous one before it dries, so that there is no overspray onto drying surfaces. The paint should be thinned as much as possible without the chance of runs - probably 70-75% thinners, unless it is a cold day. If you are good, and lucky, the final coat will only require cutting and polishing. If any paint is needed to be removed use 1000 or 1200 grade 'wet and dry' with soap to flatten it before cutting and polishing.

There was a time when all that was required on the the the underside of wings, etc. was to give them some underseal and forget them. Now this is not considered acceptable if the car is to be shown and some finish that is both durable and attractive to look at must be considered. If the car is sprayed professionally with two-pack paint this is quite chip resistant and may be sufficient for most purposes. There are, however, quite a range of chip resistant undercoats that can be sprayed under the final finish and some of these are also suitable for home application under cellulose. No paint finish will resist all attacks by stones and grit so add the occasional touching in session to the maintenance schedule.

COLOURS OF COMPONENTS ON THE MGA.

The following comes from my knowledge of MGAs gained over the years and from a study of factory photographs. Having owned at one time a low mileage, unrestored 1600 I can talk about what was original on that car but would not like to be dogmatic about every MGA as the practice at the factory changed and occasional component shortages meant that cars were assembled, from time to time, with items finished in a different manner.

Engine
As supplied to Abingdon the engine was assembled complete with dynamo, starter motor and so on already fitted. After assembly the engine was painted maroon so, in addition to the basic block, the dynamo, starter motor, water pump and pulley, the inlet manifold, heat shield and the dip stick were also maroon. In addition on the 1500 (except for some early cars where it was black) and on early 1600s, the fan was also maroon. On later 1600s and on 1600 Mk IIs this was yellow. The gearbox was added to the engine after painting so was left raw aluminium with the pressed tin cover plate painted gloss black.

The carburettors were left raw, unpolished aluminium and the air cleaners on both pushrod and twin cam cars painted in satin black.

The radiator and header tank was painted a non-gloss black, I say non-gloss rather than matt because I feel a satin finish is closer to original that the very matt finish often seen.

Chassis and Suspension.

The chassis was gloss - but not too shiny - black as were the suspension components, steering rack and the arms of the dampers. The damper bodies were left raw aluminium. The chassis extensions and the bumper mounting brackets were also gloss black.

Brake cylinders were left unpainted but brake back plates and drums were gloss black (also not too shiny).

The floorboards were sprayed black giving a matt surface appearance. However, the transmission tunnel was just given a single coat of gloss black paint which soon peeled off!

Electrical Components.

These were fitted 'as supplied' so coils, relays, etc. were unpainted with the standard raw aluminium or plated steel finish. The wiper motor body casing was a satin - nearly matt - black finish with the rest left raw aluminium.

The heater box was finished gloss black but the amount of 'gloss' varied from batch to batch. The securing clips were plated and good, new reproductions of these made from original tools are available.

Body.

When the body was painted the bonnet, doors and boot lid were already in place. It follows, therefore, that the hinges, release knobs and attendant fittings were also painted body colour.

A batch of cars leave the factory for shipping abroad. On the transporter complete, trimmed bodies have arrived.

CHAPTER NINE

TRIM AND WEATHER EQUIPMENT

After the paint finish it is the interior trim of the car that most attracts the viewer. This is particularly true of any open car and with the MGA we are fortunate that the interior is very attractive. Unlike some later M.G.s, black trim always had contrasting piping to improve the look of the interior and all the cars had leather faced seats in a range of colours that complimented the exterior finish.

I prefer sticking with the original factory options when painting and trimming a car as these schemes were, for the most part, well chosen and suit the overall design well. Particularly in hotter climates the original leather would have deteriorated and it is more than likely the car will have been re-trimmed at some time. Often the seats have been fitted with plastic covers and the best of these do look like leather. I would not like these on my car but I can see the sense if you live somewhere hot and cannot face the cost of regular replacement of dried up and cracked leather seats. I know leather can be treated with hide food to try to preserve it but I have no personal experience of trying this in a hot climate.

If any of the original trim remains, perhaps buried under replacement seat covers, this will provide a clue to the original colour. Alternatively a check with the British Motor Industry Heritage Trust at Gaydon will give the paint and trim colours of the car when it was built. To maintain originality, when changing the trim to another colour, try to chose one that would have been used with the exterior colour selected. For example, tan trim was not offered with Old English White paintwork.

On the Twin Cam, 1600 and 1600 Mk II the factory offered the option of 'de-luxe competition' seats. These were not fitted to all Twin Cams and were selected by some purchasers for pushrod cars. The seats are comfortable but for taller drivers do have the disadvantage of reducing the leg room because the back rests are thicker. Although home trimming of these seats is possible, most experts advise leaving the job to a professional as it is a lot less easy than with the standard seat. If it is decided to fit new covers at home, study the construction of the old seats carefully, particularly the way the cords from the corners of the central panel are pulled through to the base to maintain the shape.

PANEL TRIM KITS

Although the interior trim panels on an MGA are simple, and it would not be difficult to cut new panels using the old ones as patterns, I would advocate buying a trim kit as this will save considerable time which can be used more profitably elsewhere.

A trim kit comprises pairs of door panels, door pockets, scuttle panels, wheel arch panels and chassis cover panels. In addition there are lengths of piping to go under dash cappings, door cappings and rear cockpit

The trim fitted to the coupe. All of the items are available from suppliers.

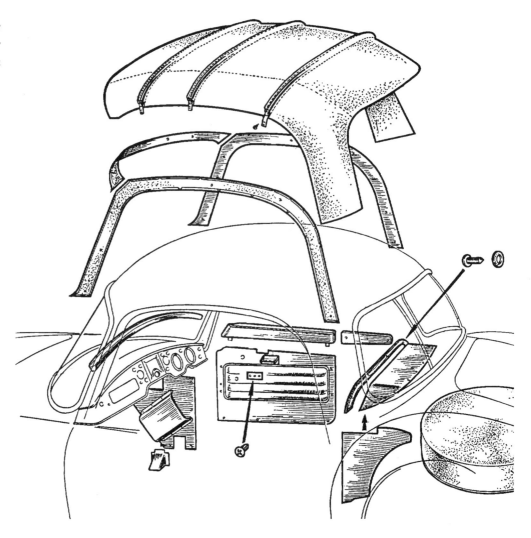

CRASH RAIL

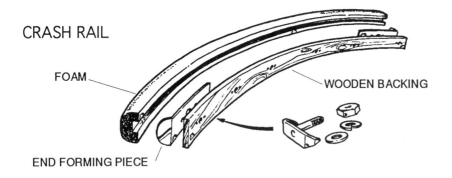

FOAM

WOODEN BACKING

END FORMING PIECE

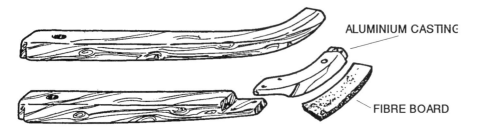

ALUMINIUM CASTING

FIBRE BOARD

EARLY ALL-WOOD DOOR CAPPING (ABOVE) AND LATER TYPE BELOW

Parts for the cockpit cappings of the roadster. Note that early cars had all-wood door capping rails but later this was replaced by rails made up of both wooden and cast aluminium sections.

A complete panel trim kit for an MGA roadster. The kit includes pairs of the main door panels, pockets, wheel arch panels and scuttle panels as well as covering material and piping for the cockpit cappings.

This small panel is used to cover the chassis brace and is held in place, once it has been folded to shape, by the side panel.

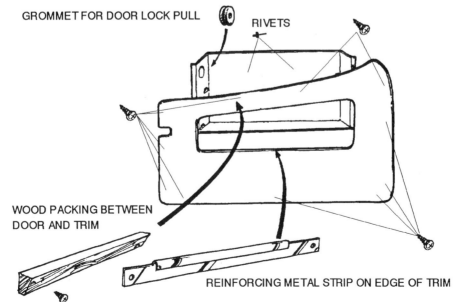

GROMMET FOR DOOR LOCK PULL

RIVETS

WOOD PACKING BETWEEN DOOR AND TRIM

REINFORCING METAL STRIP ON EDGE OF TRIM

rail. The door cappings and rear quarter cappings are leather with the crash pads, dash top and dashboard (if covered) utilising leathercloth.

The trim panels are easily fitted with self tapping screws in cup washers. The small chassis covering panels are folded to shape and are held by the side panels. There is a grommet in the rear of the door pocket for the door pull and remember to fit the packing piece to the top of the door and the 'U' shaped metal strip to the lower edge of the opening in the door trim before screwing the trim to the door. The door pocket lining is fixed to the reinforcing bar in the door with two pop rivets. To ease subsequent removal it might be easier to replace these with self tapping screws.

FITTING THE COCKPIT RAILS

This is not as easy as it looks. The earlier cars had the door capping rails made entirely of wood and the later cars had a combination of wood and aluminium. The aluminium sections had hardboard glued to the underside to accept the fastenings for the covering. The leather covering will not conceal any imperfections in these rails so it is important to make sure the joints between the aluminium and the wood are smooth. All the fixing captive bolts should be in place and the sections trial fitted to the car before removing them to apply the covering. Look to see that they all line up correctly and that there is sufficient clearance between the pieces to allow for the thicknesses of leather.

To fix the leather to the door capping this should first be attached at the rear end and worked towards the curved end, tacking or stapling, keeping the material taut. At the ends of the rails the leather is folded neatly and fastened underneath. Remove some of the excess material to stop the rail being lifted up at the ends.

The piping is attached to the outside edge and fastened underneath. Peel back the leathercloth from the inner core and cut off about half an inch (1cm.) of this inner core at the ends and turn these under to make a neat finish. When fixing the leathercloth over the foam crash rail do not try to draw this too tight. If the cloth does not seem to want to work neatly over the foam, and there are creases, try warming it a little with a hair dryer or leave it out in the sun. Note that the ends have finishing pieces to support the foam.

DASHBOARD AND SCUTTLE TOP

Where the dashboard and the scuttle top are to be covered then some dismantling is necessary if the car is still in one piece. To cover the top of the scuttle first remove the windscreen. Use a suitable contact adhesive to attach the leathercloth. Care should be taken here as the grade of adhesive may depend on the paint finish used on the car. Take advice from a specialist motor factor and try some on an out-of-the-way piece of paintwork before committing yourself. Some adhesives react with the paint and never dry satisfactorily.

The dashboard and instruments must be removed to cover the dashboard with leathercloth. After sticking with contact adhesive, use metal clips to hold the edges of the leathercloth to the rim of the dashboard.

SEATS

A decision must be made whether to repair and recover the original seats, or to replace completely. All parts of the seats are now available as separate components and it may only be necessary to clean up and paint the frame and replace the sagging seat foams with new ones before recovering. The wooden seat bases are, however, often in poor condition and it is unsatisfactory to try to fix new covers to poor bases.

The secret of any good looking seat lies beneath the cover. It is important to make sure the padding and foams are in good condition, and fit the cover well. A seat where the cover is loose will soon lose shape and the leather will crease badly. You often see cars where the piping around the top of the seat back does not line up with the top of the underlying seat structure - this is because the cover was applied over an insufficiently padded seat.

The photographic sequence on the next four pages shows the process of covering an MGA roadster seat.

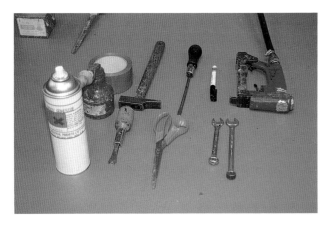

Only simple tools are needed. In the absence of a staple gun, tacks would be quite adequate. The spray can contains contact adhesive.

Pads of rubberised horse hair, seat base and foam, backboard and thin felt. These items come in the trim kit but in addition some wadding will be needed.

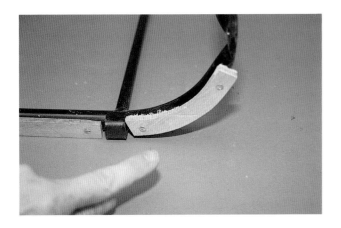

Screw tacking strips of plywood to the base of the seat back or replace the old strips on a used frame.

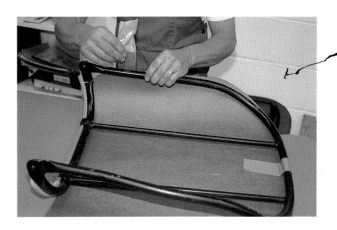

Check that only the cover and frame for one seat are worked on at a time - they are handed. Tape the backboard to the frame.

Mark out the shape of the seat back on the larger piece of rubberised horse hair and cut it to size. Separating it slightly to make two cuts will help.

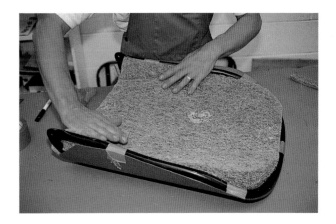

Glue the smaller pad of horse hair in the bottom centre of the larger, and place this in the frame with the smaller pad against the backboard.

To pad the edges of the seat use strips of wadding - this needs doubling up and sticking to the seat with contact adhesive.

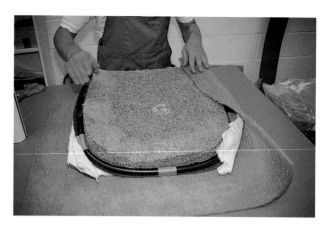

Thin felt is used to cover the back and this is placed over the wadding.

The thin felt is brought over to the front of the seat and glued with the spray-on contact adhesive. Cuts are made to reduce the bulk at the folds.

The seat back is now well padded and is ready for the seat cover.

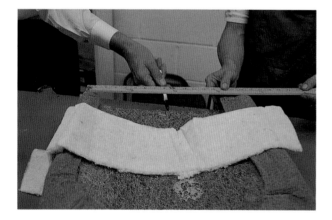

The centre of the back rest is marked so that the pleats can be lined up. The strip of wadding will be used to cover the top of the seat back.

A piece of thin plastic - part of the bag the kit came in was used here - helps the seat cover slide over the wadding.

The seat cover is carefully pulled down over the back - pulling by the side cords. Care is needed to make sure the seat cover stitching isn't strained.

The piping at the top must line up with the seat back and some working of the material will be needed to achieve this. Line centre of pleats with the mark made earlier.

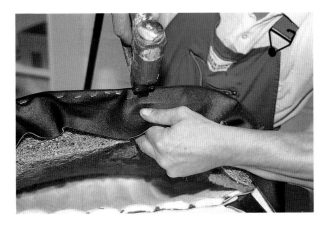

When the cover fits properly it is stapled or tacked to the ply strips on the frame - the cover is pulled down evenly to remove creases.

Spare material is cut away and the piping neatly tucked in at the corners - exposing the brackets that fix the seat back to the base.

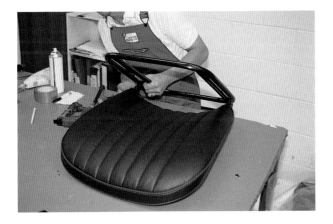

The two parts of the frame are bolted together with plated nuts and bolts.

The seat base is assembled and tried in the frame - adjust if necessary. A piece of thin felt is placed inside the metal tray and stapled to the wood.

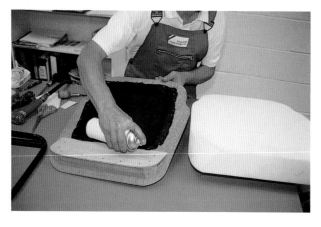

The seat foam is trimmed to the size of the base and glued in place upon it.

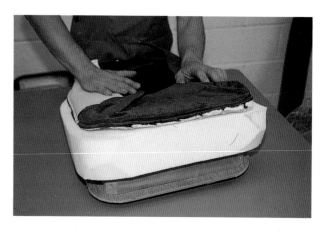

The seat cover is placed on top and the sides drawn down over the base.

The cover is pulled down all round, working the foam into place.

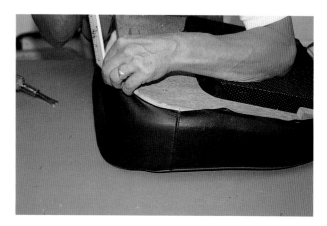

It is often necessary to use a blunt edged piece of wood to manipulate the foam.

The seat is offered up to the frame to check the centre line of the pleats - they must line up.

When the pleats align, and the sides look neat, the seat cover is stapled or pinned to the wooden base.

CARPETS

The carpets on the MGA were originally 'Karvel'. This was a bonded carpet which did not fray and for this reason only a few of the edges were bound with black leathercloth. The rear edges of the gearbox covers were bound, along with the edges of the access flap for the gearbox oil filler and the area around the cut outs for the chassis braces.

With, perhaps, the exception of some early cars, all MGA roadsters were all fitted with black carpets. Some authorities state that other colours were fitted to the early cars to tone with the upholstery but I can find no evidence of this in parts lists. All coupes seem to have had grey carpets. The carpets for both the roadster and coupe were fitted over a thin felt and if carpe similar grade to the original is chosen for the ret⎯⎯ then they will look better if fitted over felt. A thin felt is available backed with shiny black waterproof surface and I have found that this keeps its shape well and is easily installed, with the black face downwards, under the carpets. Although not original, I find that if the felt is laid before the fastenings for the carpet are fitted, and then these are fixed through the felt with a washer under the fixing to hold the felt in place, the carpets do not tend to move around as you get in and out of the car.

When fitting carpets make sure that these do not restrict the movement of the pedals or prevent the full movement of the gear lever.

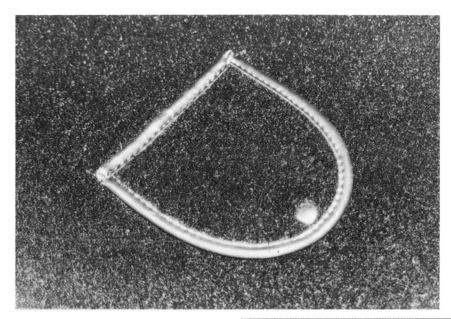

Only a few edges of the carpet were bound originally. The access flap for the gearbox filler, the section round the chassis braces and the edges of the gear box cover were bound.

Only the driver's side of the car had a heel mat. The original pattern is seen here.

The central arm rest was sewn to the tunnel carpet and this does require a heavy duty sewing machine. Some suppliers now sell the armrest separate from the carpet and advise that this be held in place with clips or velcro. Personally I would find someone with a suitable machine to fix the armrest in place.

Although only the back board behind the seats on the roadster was carpeted originally, it is the practice now to also cover the battery compartment lid with carpet and this obviously looks better. Some suppliersl also sell carpet sets for the boot (trunk) but I would want to be certain the boot lid did not leak before fitting one of these.

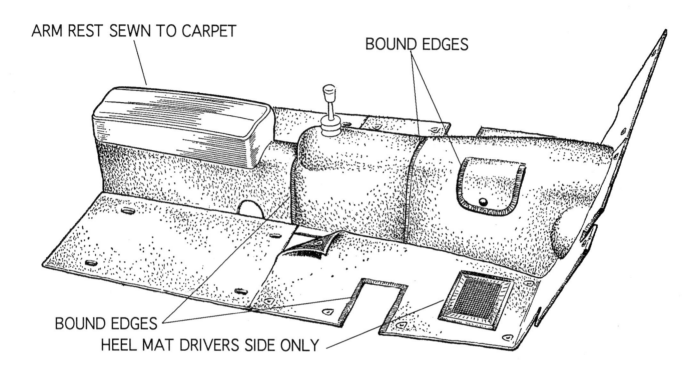

ARM REST SEWN TO CARPET

BOUND EDGES

BOUND EDGES
HEEL MAT DRIVERS SIDE ONLY

TONNEAU COVER

There were two styles of cover supplied with MGAs. All 1500s, except those built in the last few months of production, had covers with a sewn-in pocket for the steering wheel. The cover was clipped to the door, as well as the scuttle and rear deck. Late 1500s and all 1600s had covers without a pocket for the steering wheel or fastenings along the top of the door.

1500s had black tonneau covers for the most part, with the exception of some cars that had Ice Blue. 1600s and 1600 Mk II covers were either grey, beige or light blue. Unfortunately, at the time of writing, neither Ice Blue (a light, slightly greenish colour) or light blue are available in Everflex - the only blue produced is far too dark although it can be used in the absence of the correct colours. The hope is that one day an enterprising supplier will commission the production of a quantity of the correct colour material.

Tonneau covers are usually supplied without the fixings attached and are simple to install. If all the studs are fitted to the car, lay the cover in place and check it for size (this really can only be done with an assistant). Make sure it will reach all the fastenings before starting to fix any of the fittings to the cover - sometimes these covers are made so the fastenings come very close to the sewn edges and it is as well to check this before punching any holes in the wrong place.

Using chalk, mark the centre of the rear edge of the cover and check that the zip is at the centre of the front. If the zip is not exactly central this does not really matter as long as you are aware of this when placing the front fixings.

From the centre line mark the position of the two inner rear studs and fix the two 'lift the dot' fasteners in place.

The spare wheel cover on all roadsters and on the 1500 coupe was made partly from grey "hardura" and partly from carpet. The edges round the aperture between the boot and rear of the cockpit were stiffened with mill board.

The stiffening round the edges of the carpet can be seen here. On the 1600 coupes the spare wheel was entirely within the boot and covered with just a grey "hardura" cover.

Fitting the fasteners to the hood and tonneau cover are easier if the correct tools are used. The tools here are old friends and were originally used in the Abingdon trim shop in the 1950s! However, many specialist trim suppliers still sell these tools. Two of the punches are designed to produce both the centre holes and the slots for the tags of 'lift the dot' fasteners.

The task is much easier if the correct punch is used and this is available from specialist tool suppliers. If the correct tool is not available then punch the centre hole with an eyelet punch and the slits for the prongs of the fastener with the point of a Stanley knife. With the rear of the cover now fastened to the two rear studs it can be pulled tight and the position of the centre scuttle studs marked, and the fastenings fitted to the cover. From this point it is just a matter of working round the rest of the fastenings, one at a time, keeping the cover tight each time when marking their positions.

If the tonneau cover zip is metal then it helps to keep it working well if a very small amount of lubricant, such as 'Vaseline' or 'Waxoyl' is applied - not enough to stain the cover though!

TONNEAU COVERS

THE EARLY STYLE TONNEAU COVER

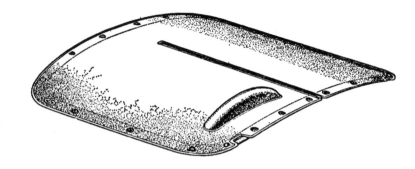

LATER STYLE COVER WITHOUT WHEEL POCKET OR DOOR FIXING

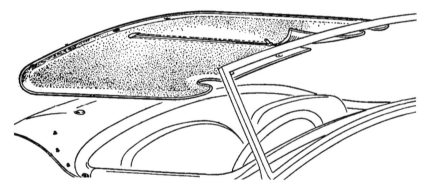

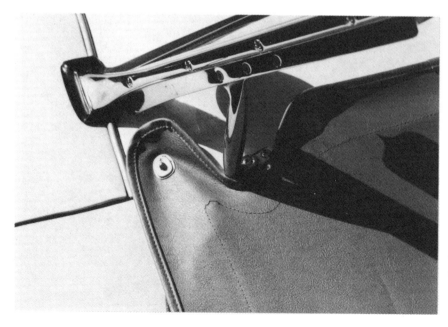

The later tonneau covers did not have fixings on the top of the door and the front had a different shape. Here it is seen that the front fixing was arranged to tension the side of the cover.

HOOD

As with the tonneau cover, not all the colours used originally are available. A number of the parts suppliers offer replacement hoods and most of these are to the later pattern with three rear windows. The early 1500s had just a single window but for better vision most cars are now fitted with the later hoods.

The process of fitting the hood is easy provided it has been made correctly. As with most things the quality varies from supplier to supplier and I can only say that if a hood looks poorly made when it is purchased then return if before trying to fit it and look elsewhere!

Unfortunately there is very little adjustment available in the windscreen frame, sidescreens and hood frame but there is a little. The sidescreens can be bent and twisted carefully to adjust fits and the angle of rake of the windscreen adjusted slightly by adding packing under the grab handles. Slackening the fixings bolts for the hood frame will allow some repositioning.

The first job is to make sure the wooden front rail is in good condition and fits the screen frame well. A good front rail will have slightly less curve than the screen frame so that when the sides are pushed down on the

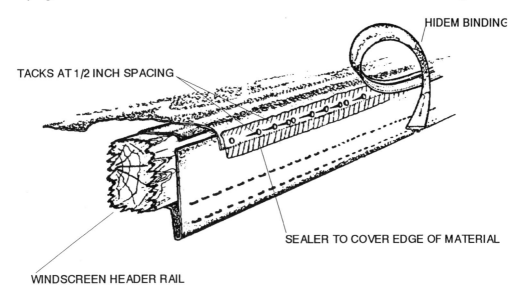

TACKS AT 1/2 INCH SPACING

HIDEM BINDING

SEALER TO COVER EDGE OF MATERIAL

WINDSCREEN HEADER RAIL

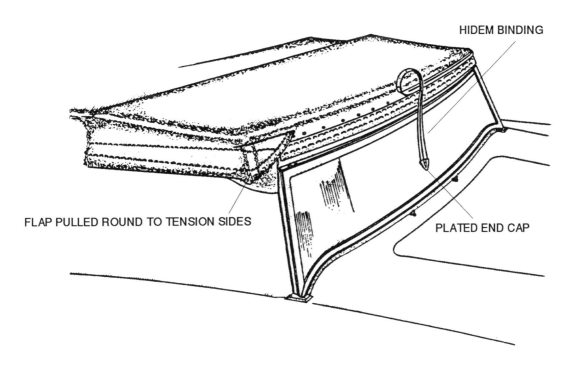

HIDEM BINDING

FLAP PULLED ROUND TO TENSION SIDES

PLATED END CAP

pegs, and the wing nuts fastened, the centre of the rail is pressing against the windscreen rail. On the later cars the factory fitted a central catch here to hold the wooden rail to the screen.

With the frame erect and the wooden front rail screwed to it, ensure the frame lines up with the screen. Adjust this as far as possible to obtain a good fit. The hood must not twist the windscreen or the glass may break.

The Everflex hood material works best when warm so fitting the hood should be done on a warm day, or with a good temperature in the garage, and the material pre-warmed in the sun or in a warm room. The first job is to fix the covering round the wooden rail. With the hood will be a piece of hood material that has been sewn

to provide the flap that comes down over the top of the windscreen frame.

Trial fit this material and mark the centre position on both this and the wooden rail. Eventually holes will need to be cut for the screen pegs to fit but I find it better to leave them until later. If the wooden header rail is not a good fit to the top of the screen then consider gluing some very thin foam or rubber to it before covering.

The covering is glued to the rail with contact adhesive making sure the front flap is correctly positioned. The join is on the top of the rail. The ends should be neatly finished off and holes for the wing nuts cut. With these in place locate the position of the holes for the windscreen pegs and cut these in the material and fix the two bronze

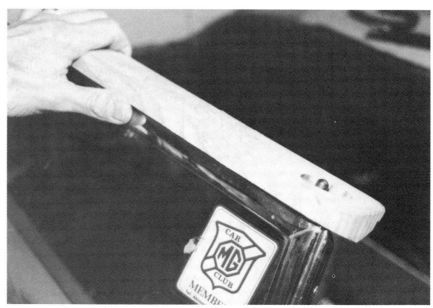

The front wooden rail must be a good fit to the top of the windscreen frame. There is little use in expecting a poorly shaped rail to seat well and keep out the rain.

With care it is possible to achieve a good fit using a ready-made hood but the result will depend much on the quality of the hood purchased.

sockets making sure they line up with the wing nuts. Clip the frame to the windscreen to make sure it fits well and trim off any surplus material from the top of the rail.

Mark the centre of the hood at front and rear, and the centre point of the front rail and rear deck. If it is not already in place, slide the metal hood retaining strip into the pocket at the rear of the hood and check that the two slots in the fabric line up with the hood fixings on deck checking the centre marks line up. The seam above the rear window must line up with the rear hood frame. Later this will be attached to the hood with chromed set screws and nuts. Pull the material to the front and line up the centre marks. Lightly tack at the front of the rail keeping the material taut. Do this across all but the last four inches of rail on each side but do not trim off any surplus fabric. If the hood looks right, mark and fit the 'lift the dot' fastenings working on each side alternately making sure the rear window is not pulled out of shape.

The plates for the side turnbuckle fastenings are then fitted to the outside layer of the hood and the fit around the sidescreens examined. If the hood material on the roof still looks tight and wrinkle free, then pull the side of the hood round the front rail to remove any bulges above the sidescreens. Try to keep a nice line along the edges without any unsightly gaps and fix these sides to the front edge of the wooden rail. Make sure all the tacks and the edge of the material can be covered by the strip of 'hidem' binding included with the hood.

To make a really water tight seal, fix more tacks along the edge so that they are about half an inch (1 cm) apart. Seal the edge of the hood and the tops of these tacks with a suitable clear sealer keeping to the area that will be under the 'hidem' binding.

Fix the 'hidem' binding with tacks over the join, concealing the tacks within the folds of the binding, and screw or pin the metal end caps in place using plated brass screws or plated pins. The final job is to fix those two plated set screws and cup washers to hold the hood material to the rear hoop of the hood frame on the line of the stitching above the rear windows.

The 1500 with the earlier type of sidescreen. The drawing on the right illustrates the different types of sidescreen fixings with the 1500 "half wing nut" followed on the right by the 1600 knurled nut.

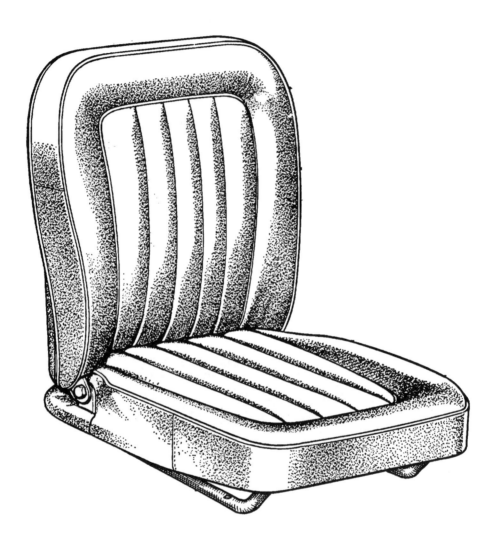

The competition seat was offered as an optional extra on the Twin Cam and both 1600 models.

CHAPTER TEN

LITERATURE AND ACCESSORIES

When the advertising agency dealing with the British Motor Corporation account were faced with selling an entirely new M.G., after many years of dealing with cars that still looked very much the same as those built ten years earlier, they really tried very hard. The slogan for the campaign was "First of a new line" and the posters, advertisements in magazines and the sales brochures all repeated the theme.

The London launch for the dealers was held at University Motors and a car finished in Old English White was displayed on a raised platform under a banner reading *"First of a new line. The completely new MGA - profiled for performance"* and it received enthusiastic acclaim from them, according to a report in the "Nuffield News Exchange" - the company magazine for dealers.

Collecting the period literature is part of the enjoyment of owning an older vehicle and we are lucky with the MGA that this is still fairly readily available from specialist dealers. The original launch theme of "First of a new line" was used in the sales brochures for quite a number of years and, indeed, it was not changed until 1958 when a new 1500 brochure was printed. The first brochures had a yellow background and were put out in a number of different versions - I have eight and I know there were many more. The earliest I have is numbered 5555 H & E, which would have been issued in 1955, and the last H & E 58-35 which dates it as early 1958. The second type of 1500 brochure (H5811 and E5812)

featured a green car on the white cover with an elegantly dressed model wearing sun glasses.

When the Twin Cam was announced a separate four page brochure was produced but the advertising agency seemed to have used a picture of a standard car on the cover with the wheels retouched! There are at at least five versions of this - I have E5836, H5837, E5838, H5884 and H59-95. The last of these reflects the changes for the second series Twin Cam.

The increased power and the disc brakes on the 1600 merited a completely new brochure which used colour photographs, rather than the drawings found in the early 1500 brochure. I have three variants of this - H5956, E5964 and H6091. As with all the other brochures there were also foreign language versions - many of which were overprinted in the country where the cars were sold. The Mark ll also merited a new brochure, H6120, together with an announcement folder H6007.

When the proud new owner collected their new MGA there was an envelope in it which was to be handed to them unopened. This contained the warranty, a schedule of repair charges for home market cars, the handbook, the service voucher book and a list of approved accessories. Luckily the Twin Cam Group of the M.G. Car Club have had a limited number of these packs reprinted for collectors as few of those issued originally survive. Whilst mentioning these it is also worth saying that both this group, and the MGA Register of the club, produce a number of very worthwhile publications of help to owners as well as running some very useful restoration seminars. Joining the club is well worth while and I have had a lot of enjoyment from my 32 years of membership!

On the subject of accessories it is often forgotten by restorers in search of "originality" that a lot of cars were delivered with many extra bits and pieces fitted. A study of the lists gives some idea of parts available but in addition many dealers would fit other contemporary parts that were sold by accessory suppliers. Very few cars in the 1950s ran without any extras and some items, like luggage racks, had almost universal appeal.

When choosing accessories to fit on a car, the golden rule is that one should only fit parts that were available when the car was new. Radios are a case in point. A modern radio looks out of place and there are now specialists who will convert a period radio to modern specification internally, whilst retaining the authentic 1950s facia. This gives the best of both worlds and the cost is not all that high - around £140 at the time of writing.

The factory issued a number of publications on improving the performance of the cars as well as service bulletins to dealers. Although there is not space to reproduce all of these here I have included some of the information they contained.

The press kits for all the MGAs were impressive. The kit here was issued for the Twin Cam and, in addition to pages of data from the Nuffield Organisation, there were a number of press photographs and a copy of the sales brochure. For those journalists lucky enough to attend the launch at the Chobham Test Track, there was a map of the circuit in case they became lost! The Twin Cam Group publish replicas of the press kit but not of the outer wallet.

Service books were included in the envelope which should have been handed unopened to the new owner. The literature pictured here is a reproduction set produced by the Twin Cam Group of the M.G. Car Club for sale to owners. Also in every new MGA sold there was a brochure inviting the buyer to join the M.G. Car Club, which then had factory support.

ACCESSORY LIST

Description	Part No.	Retail Price
		£ s. d.
1. Fog lamp	ADH785	3 15 0
Brackets for fog & driving lamps (R.H.)	AHH5521	2 11 8
Brackets for fog & driving lamps (L.H.)	AHH5520	2 11 8
2. Radiator blind	AHH5536	3 15 0
3. Driving lamp	17H5322	4 2 6
4. Wing mirror	27H9680	1 1 6
5. External luggage carrier	AHH5495	11 15 0
6. Windscreen washers	AHH5983	1 10 0
7. Travelling-rug (all-wool tartan) ..	27H9635	2 19 6
Tartans available { Anderson / Buchanan / Davidson of Tulloch / Dress Stewart / Macbeth / Macgregor / Macleod / Royal Stewart / Wallace		
8. Heater	AHH5422	15 15 0
9. Seat covers	According to material	8 0 0 (av. price)
10. Horn (high note)	1B9008	2 5 0
11. Paint pencil	According to colour	4 9
12. Battery filler bottle	97H2510	8 6
13. Fire extinguisher (5½″ × 1½″)	97H752	1 19 6
Fire extinguisher (9½″ × 1½″)	97H753	2 15 0
14. Polishing mitt	97H698	13 7
15. Foot pump	2H3570	1 10 9
16. Exhaust deflector	97H602	15 9
17. Reversing lamp	97H2150	1 10 0
Illuminating switch	57H5172	10 0

B.M.C. Underbody Seal: For additional protection at reasonable charges B.M.C. Underbody Seal is recommended. Consult your M.G. Dealer for full details.

The car above has been fitted with quite a number of period accessories. In addition to the hard top, which is the later glassfibre type, the car has a luggage rack, headlamp 'eyebrows' to make short work of any unlucky pedestrians in the way, and a wing mirror.

The page from the service book shows just how inexpensive running an MGA looks after over 30 years of British inflation.

12,000 MILES   £6·5·1

1. **ENGINE.** Remove carburetter suction chambers and pistons, clean, re-assemble and top up.
Remove carburetter float chambers, empty sediment and re-fit.
Lubricate carburetter controls.
Check valve rocker clearances and adjust if necessary.
Clean and re-oil air filter elements.
Check dynamo drive belt tension.
Lubricate water pump sparingly.
Clean fuel pump filter.
2. **IGNITION.** Check automatic ignition control, lubricating drive shaft, cam and advance mechanism.
Clean and adjust distributor contact points.
Fit new sparking plugs.
3. **CLUTCH.** Check level of fluid in the hydraulic clutch supply tank and top up if necessary.
4. **STEERING.** Check steering and suspension moving parts for wear.
5. **BRAKES.** Check brakes, adjust if necessary.
Make visual inspection of brake lines and pipes.
Check level of fluid in the hydraulic brake supply tank and top up if necessary.
Inspect disc brake friction pads and report if adjustment is required.
6. **HYDRAULIC DAMPERS.** Examine

all hydraulic dampers for leaks and top up if necessary.
7. **RADIATOR.** Drain, flush out and refill radiator.
8. **GENERAL.** Tighten rear road spring seat bolts.
9. **BODY.** Check and tighten if necessary door hinges and striker plate securing screws.
Lubricate door hinges, door locks, bonnet lock and operating mechanism.
10. **ELECTRICAL.** Check battery cell specific gravity readings and top up to correct level.
Lubricate dynamo bearing.
11. **LUBRICATION.** Drain engine, flush out and refill with fresh oil.*
Change oil in gearbox and rear axle.
Fit new oil filter element.
Lubricate all grease nipples.
Re-pack front hub caps with grease.
Lubricate speedometer and revolution indicator cables.
Lubricate rack and pinion.
12. **WHEELS AND TYRES.** Change road wheels round diagonally, including spare, to regularise tyre wear. Check tyre pressures. Check wheel alignment.
13. **HEADLAMPS.** Check beam setting and adjust if necessary.
14. **TEST.** Road test car and report.

* *Remove engine sump, clean out, refit and refill with fresh oil at 24,000 miles.*
See Schedule of Repair Charges for price.
Pt. Nos. Brake and clutch fluid : 17H7847 (1 qt.).
Sparking plugs : 3H2006.   Oil filter element : 8G683.

All new MGAs were sent out with the spare ignition key fitted in a leather key fob. The leather matched the colour of the upholtery. Unfortunately not many survived with the cars.

The reverse of the key fob was gold printed "Real English leather is used in this upholstery".

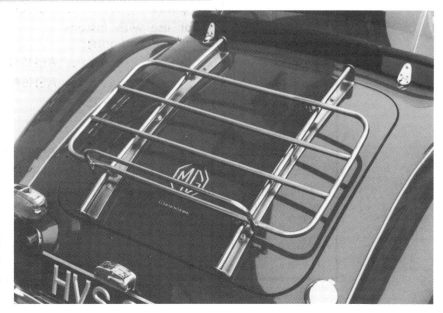

The luggage rack was a near essential for any serious touring, but the boot lid was often distorted by overloading.

Racing and Competition Equipment

	Part No.	
	'MGA 1500'	'MGA 1600'
Fuel tank—15 gal.		AHH5863
Fuel gauge—15 gal.		17H299
Tank unit—15 gal.		BHA4094
Fuel tank—17 gal.		AHH5990
Fuel gauge—17 gal.		BHA5159
Tank unit—17 gal.		BHA4161
Tank strap assembly (qty. 2)		AHH5999
Bracket—front tank mounting		AHH5501
Rear hanger—tank strap		AHH5502
Windshield—full-width (aluminium and perspex)..	AFH2591	AFH2591
Steering-wheel (wood rim, light alloy, Italian)	AHH5800	AHH5800
Exhaust valve (high-duty)	1H1025	1H1025
Piston assembly — flat head — 9·0 : 1 ratio	1H1178	
Piston assembly—raised head—10·1 : 1, including:	1H1180	
Piston rings	1H1181	
Gudgeon pin	1H1110	
Circlip—gudgeon pin	CCN214	
Connecting rods (for use with pistons having fully floating gudgeon pins):		
Nos. 2 and 4	AEH642	AEH642
Nos. 1 and 3	AEH644	AEH644
Piston assembly — flat head — 9·25 : 1 ratio		12H173
Carburetters—1¾ in. (44·45 mm.) (1 pair)	AUC780	AUC780
Gasket—carburetter—1¾ in. (44·45 mm.)	AHH5791	AHH5791
Inlet manifold for 1¾ in. (44·45 mm.) carburetters	AEH200	AEH200
Valve springs (outer)	1H1111	1H1111
Valve springs (inner)	1H1112	1H1112

Racing and Competition Equipment—*continued*

		Part No.	
		'MGA 1500'	'MGA 1600'
First motion shaft—gearbox	⎫	1H3297	1H3297
Laygear	⎬ close-ratio gearbox	1H3298	1H3298
Second speed mainshaft gear		1H3299	1H3299
Third speed mainshaft gear	⎭	1H3300	1H3300
Competition clutch assembly (extra-high-duty)		AHH5457	AHH5457
Crown wheel and pinion (10/41)—4·1 : 1 ratio		ATB7240	ATB7240
Speedometer for 4·1 : 1 ratio rear axle (m.p.h.)		BHA4060	BHA4060
Speedometer for 4·1 : 1 ratio rear axle (km.p.h.)		BHA4061	BHA4061
Crown wheel and pinion (11/43)—3·9 : 1 ratio		ATB7236	ATB7236
Speedometer for 3·9 : 1 ratio rear axle (m.p.h.)		BHA4068	BHA4068
Speedometer for 3·9 : 1 ratio rear axle (km.p.h.)		BHA4069	BHA4069
Crown wheel and pinion (9/41)—4·55 : 1 ratio		ATB7146	ATB7146
Speedometer for 4·55 : 1 ratio rear axle (m.p.h.)		17H295	17H295
Speedometer for 4·55 : 1 ratio rear axle (km.p.h.)		17H296	17H296
Oil cooler kit		8G2282	8G2282
Bonnet straps and plates		AHH5518/9	AHH5518/9
Wire wheels (60-spoke with 4½ in. aluminium alloy rims, 15 in. diameter) ..		AHH8000	AHH8000
Wire wheels (60-spoke with 4½ in. steel rims, 15 in. diameter)		AHH8001	AHH8001
Brake-shoe lined assembly (lined with Ferodo VG95/1 competition facings)		8G8215	
Brake linings (VG95/1) and rivets ..		AHH5604	
Blanking sleeve (thermostat by-pass) ..		11G176	11G176

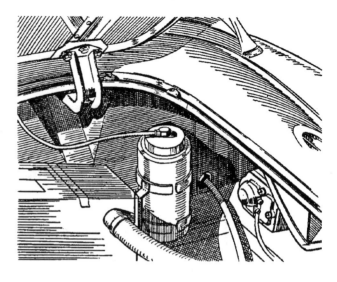

Winscreen washer early 1500 (above) and Twin Cam (below)

Windscreen washer later cars

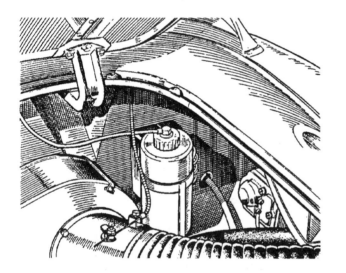

WINDSCREEN WASHERS

These were always listed as optional extras for the MGA and some cars were fitted with non factory style units. On factory equipped cars both the style of bottle, and its position, was changed during the production run. The earlier bottle had a smaller neck and lid as is clearly shown in these drawings.

A later style bottle and lid on a restored car.

Engine bay of a restored 1600 coupe. Not seen here is the sound deadening pad that was fitted under the scuttle of the coupe models but not of the roadsters.

A period H.M.V. radio. It is possible to have period car radios fitted with modern internal parts so that VHF transmissions can be received.

The optional competition fuel tank and twin fuel pumps on this ex-works MGA.

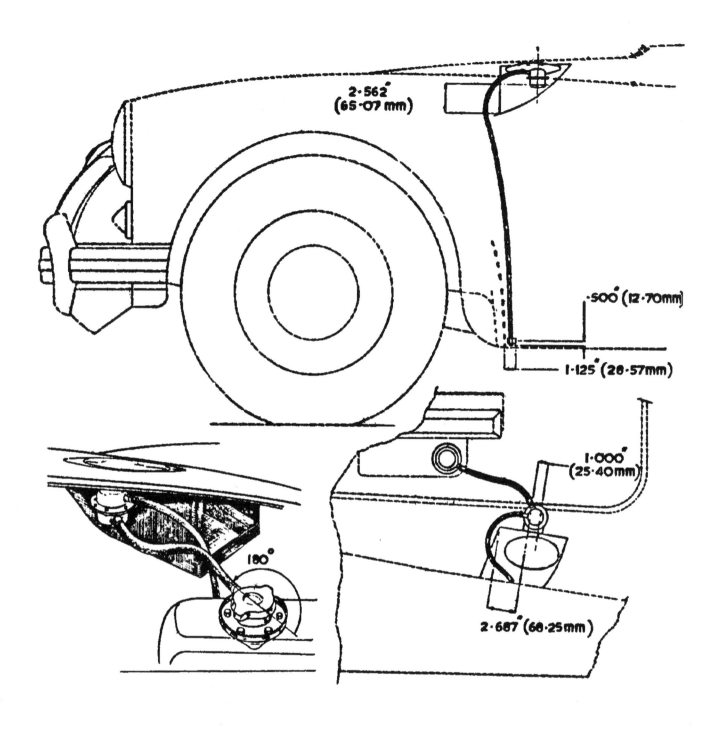

WATER LOSS - TWIN CAM

To rectify a problem with water loss, owing to vibration of the header tank pressure cap, the factory issued a service bulletin instructing dealers to fit a 7 lb. valve to the side of the engine compartment and to replace the existing cap with a plain one, without a pressure release valve. In addition to the pressure valve (part No. AHH5904), they listed the parts needed as a hose (AHH5905), bracket for valve (AHH5906), overflow pipe (AHH5907) and plain filler cap (AHH5904) in addition to sundry nuts, bolts, washers and clips. The filler neck on the header tank was rotated 180 degrees, the bracket was mounted on the air duct under the wing and a hole drilled for the overflow pipe. By now most Twin Cams will have been converted but the drawing above gives the details for any that may have escaped.

The water pressure release valve on a Twin Cam. The overflow pipe can just be seen.

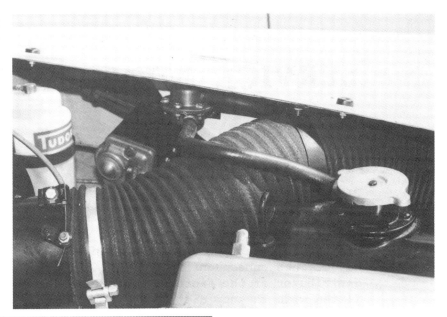

The water and air flow valves on a Twin Cam heater.

The Twin Cam heater. The casing is quite different from the type fitted to pushrod cars. This is an earlier car with the 1500 style lights. The relay for the flasher is mounted on the bulkhead next to the flasher unit.

SERVICE MEMORANDUM

28 January 1960

<u>PISTON FAILURE</u>   'MGA' Twin—Cam

To prevent the possibility of piston failure, a new
distributor, Part No. AEJ41, was introduced at Engine No. 2222.
All engines subsequent to that No. will be fitted with the new
distributor at the Factory. The following engines also were
fitted with the new distributor:

2028	2040	2200 to 2206)	
2029	2041	2209 to 2219)	inclusive.
2038	2188		

In the event of piston failure occurring with an engine
prior to the above numbers, the new distributor should be
fitted when the pistons are changed. As the new distributor
does not have a vacuum advance mechanism, the vacuum pipe
(carburetter to distributor) should be discarded and the
tapping in the carburetter blanked-off with a plug
(Part No. AUC1289).

Before fitting the new distributor, it is most important
to ensure that there is no excessive backlash in the
distributor drive gears. This check should be carried out as
follows:-

1.   Remove header tank hose to gain access to distributor.

2.   Remove distributor cap and rotor arm.

3.   Lock up automatic advance mechanism of
     distributor by removing screw 'A'
     (Fig. 1) from centre spindle and
     refitting it with a washer 'B'. This
     washer should be made from a length of
     wire .030" (.76 mm.) diameter and $1\frac{1}{8}$"
     (28.57 mm.) long, bent to form a circle.

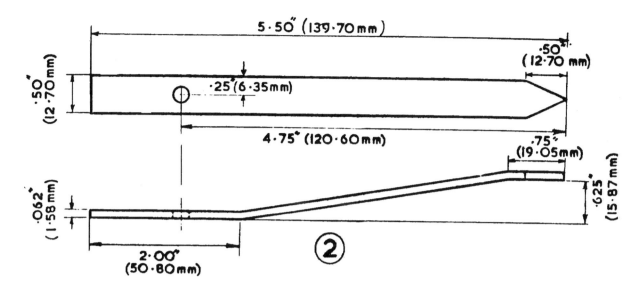

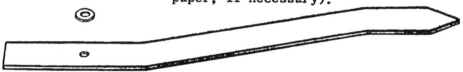

4. Make up a pointer (as shown in Fig. 2) and attach it to a disused rotor arm by drilling through centre of rotor and fitting nut & bolt (Fig. 3).

5. Fit rotor and pointer to distributor, ensuring that the rotor is really tight on the spindle (by wedging with a piece of paper, if necessary).

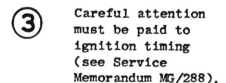

6. The pointer should now be turned so that it is over flange of camshaft cover (see Fig. 4) and then tightened on the rotor arm. The backlash in distributor drive gears is now indicated by the maximum movement of pointer. Turn pointer anti-clockwise and mark position of end of pointer on flange; then turn pointer clockwise and mark again (see 'A' Fig 4).

If distance between the two marks exceeds $\frac{5}{16}$" (8 mm.), distributor drive gears must be renewed before new distributor is fitted.

Careful attention must be paid to ignition timing (see Service Memorandum MG/288).

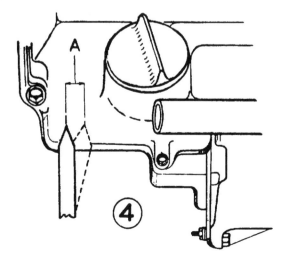

SERVICE MEMORANDUM

29 Sept. 1960

TIMING CHAIN TENSIONER

MGA
MGA 1600

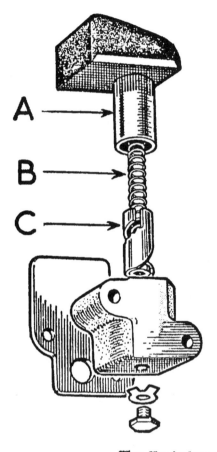

A →

B →

C →

The slipper head assembly of the timing chain tensioner fitted to the above *is* now offered as a service part under Part No. 17H31

This assembly, which consists of the slipper head ('A' in sketch), spring 'B' and plunger 'C', may be used as a replacement in the original body, provided that the latter is not damaged or unduly worn.

If the mouth of the bore of the body has worn oval by more than .003" (.76 mm.), then the body should be scrapped and a complete new tensioner fitted.

The Workshop Manuals give full instructions on removing and dismantling these units.

SERVICE MEMORANDUM

MGF/79

18 July 1961

DISC BRAKES   MGA 1600

Excessive inner pad wear may be alleviated by fitting dust covers to the brake discs as shown.

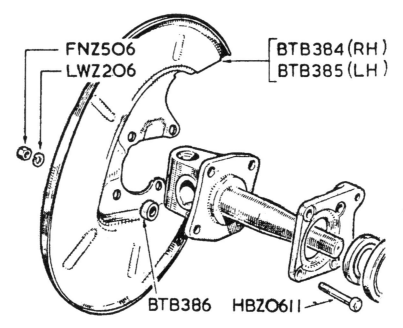

Parts required are as follows:

Description	Part No.	No. off per car
Disc dust cover R/H	BTB384	1 off
Disc dust cover L/H	BTB385	1 off
Distance washer	BTB386	8 off
Bolt	HBZ0611	8 off
Nut	FNZ506	8 off
Spring washer	LWZ206	8 off

Remove the front hub assembly as detailed in the Workshop Manual (Section KK1).

Replace the existing adaptor plate bolts with Part No. HBZ0611.

Assemble distance washer Part No. BTB386 to each bolt as shown, fit the appropriate disc dust cover and assemble with new spring washers Part No. FNZ506 and nuts LWZ206, ensuring that the nuts are tightened to 35 - 40 lbs. ft. (4.83 - 5.52 kg. m.) torque.

Reassemble the front hub as detailed in the Workshop Manual (Section KK2).

When replacing the brake caliper it is essential that the caliper securing bolts are tightened to 45 - 50 lbs. ft. (6.22 - 6.91 kg. m.).

SERVICE MEMORANDUM

22 Nov. 1960

HARD TOP AND SLIDING SIDESCREENS

MGA 1500
MGA 1600
MGA Twin-Cam

The aluminium hard top assembly, Part No. AHH5562, is no longer available and a fibre-glass (black Vynide-covered) type, Part No. AHH5991, will be offered in its place.

To ensure that the correct type of sliding sidescreen is used, refer to the chart below:

MODEL	TYPE OF HARD/SOFT TOP FITTED	SLIDING SIDESCREEN Part No.
MGA 1500 MGA 1600 MGA Twin Cam	Fibre-glass hard top	AHH5984 (R/H) AHH5985 (L/H)
MGA 1500 MGA 1600 MGA Twin Cam	Aluminium hard top	AHH5731 (R/H) AHH5732 (L/H)
MGA 1500	Soft top	AHH5731 (R/H) AHH5732 (L/H)
MGA 1600	Soft top	AHH5984 (R/H) AHH5985 (L/H)
MGA Twin Cam	Soft top (prior to Car No. 2193)	AHH5731 (R/H) AHH5732 (L/H)
MGA Twin Cam	Soft top (from Car No. 2193)	AHH5984 (R/H) AHH5985 (L/H)

SERVICE MEMORANDUM

2 July 1962

WINDSCREEN RE-GLAZING
(CONVERTIBLES ONLY)

MGA
MGA 1600
MGA 1600 (Mark II)
MGA TWIN-CAM

When reglazing the screens on these models the following precautions should be taken. (See also Section S.12 of Workshop Manual AKD600):

1. Ensure that frame top and bottom members follow contour of glass. If necessary bend them to suit.

2. Assemble frame initially without glass to ensure that corner stiffening brackets are bent to correct angles, that all securing screws fit properly and that the mitred corners are correctly aligned.

3. Discard wooden packing piece previously used and fit a single thickness of rubber strip 24B503 cut to 40" (1 metre) to support screen in lower part of frame. Ensure rubber DOES NOT OVERLAP corner stiffening brackets.

4. Use correct spongy type of glazing rubber, Part No. AFH1724.

5. Check that corners are correctly aligned and all screws are tight.

6. Ensure that screws holding screen to stanchions can be inserted without any distortion or bending. If necessary, adjust packings or the angle of the stanchion.

7. Check that the longer of the four screws ($\frac{3}{4}$"; 19 mm.) is refitted in the BOTTOM hole in stanchion.

8. To ensure that stanchions are not stressed it may be necessary to pack the grab handle or slightly reposition its fixing holes on the scuttle.

9. Check that hood front rail fits screen correctly without distortion.

10. Ensure that sidescreens do not force windscreen out of position when doors are closed.

USEFUL ADDRESSES

Anglo Parts N.V.
Brusselsesteenweg 245,
B-2800 Mechelen,
Belgium.
Tel: (015) 42 37 83
Fax: (015) 42 34 45
All parts including rebuilt body shells.

Ashley Hinton,
Unit 36,
Bookham Industrial Park,
Church Road,
Bookham,
Surrey KT23 3EU.
Tel: (01372) 456304
Fax: (01372) 456477
Heaters.

Brown & Gammons Ltd.
18, High Street,
Baldock,
Herts SG7 6AS
Tel: (01462) 490049
Fax: (01462) 896167
Parts, mechanical and bodywork restoration.
Competition parts and advice.

Burlen Fuel Systems Ltd.,
Spitfire House, Castle Road,
Salisbury,
Wilts SP1 3SA.
Tel: (01722) 412500
Fax: (01722) 334221.
All SU carburettors and fuel pumps.

Clarke Spares & Restoration,
90, West Swamp Road,
Doylestown,
PA. 18901, USA.
Tel: (215) 348 4160
Embossed engine ID plates to original pattern.

Wm. M. Collingburn,
Kimber House,
Lombard's Wynd,
Richmond,
North Yorks DL10 4JY
Tel: (01748) 824105
Trim.

Merton Motorsport (Gerry Brown),
Merton Farmhouse,
Dallinghoo,
Woodbridge,
Suffolk IP13 0LE.
Tel: (01473) 737256 Fax: (01473) 737798
Mechanical restoration. Race and rally preparation.

**MG Car Club MGA Register and MG Car Club
Twin Cam Group,**
Kimber House,
P.O. Box 251,
Abingdon,
Oxon OX14 1FF
Tel: (01235) 555552
Fax: (01235) 533755
Monthly magazine, events and technical help.

MG Owners Club
Freepost,
Cambridge, CB4 1BR
Tel: (01954) 31125
Fax: (01954) 32106

Moss Darlington,
15, Allington Way,
Yarm Road Ind. Estate,
Darlington,
Co. Durham DL1 4QB.
Tel: (01325) 281343
Fax: (01325) 485563
Parts.

Moss (USA),
P.O. Box 847,
7200 Hollister Ave.,
Goleta,
Ca. 93117, U.S.A.
Tel: (toll free US & Canada)
800 235 6954
Fax: (805) 968 6910.
Parts.

Newton Commercial Ltd.,
Eastlands Ind. Estate, Leiston,
Suffolk IP16 4LL.
Tel: (01728) 832880.
Fax: (01728) 832881.
Trim kits, Seat covers, Carpet sets.

North American MGA Reg.
Bill Gallihugh,
2114, Pinehurst Drive,
Carmel,
In. 46032, USA.

NTG Motor Services,
282-284, Bramford Road,
Ipswich,
Suffolk IP1 4AY.
Tel: (01473) 211240
Fax: (01473) 743133.
Parts

S.U. Midel Pty. Ltd.,
4, Frazer Street,
Lakemba,
NSW, Australia.
Tel: 61 2 759 5598
Fax: 61 2 758 1155
Carburettors and fuel pumps.

T & J Enterprises,
P.O. Box 1963,
Hall Green,
Birmingham B28 9LP.
Tel: 0121 777 3386
Obsolete Lucas specialist.

Vintage Radio Services,
37 Court Road,
Frampton Cotterell,
Bristol,
BS17 2DE
Tel: (01454) 772814
Suppliers and restorers of car radios.

Vintage Restorations,
The Old Bakery,
Windmill Street,
Tunbridge Wells,
Kent TN2 4UU.
Tel: (01892) 525899
Fax: (01892) 525499
Instruments.

Peter Wood,
Westwood,
Portway,
Portway Road,
Twyford,
Bucks, MK18 4EB.
Tel: (01296) 730310
Fax: (01296) 738499
Restoration - Specialist on the Twin Cam.

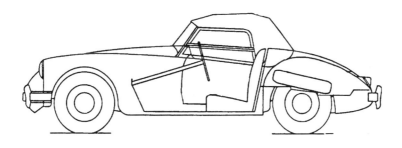

PHOTOGRAPH CREDITS

All photographs are by the author, or from his collection, except those listed below:

Jan v d Heijden 51 (bottom), 53 (centre), 54 (bottom), 55 and 59 (top).
Gerry Brown 76 and 77.

The Charlwood cartoon on page 20 was originally printed in *Safety Fast!* and is reproduced from the original drawing which is in the author's collection.

INDEX

BRITISH MOTOR HERITAGE

MG MGA SERIES
OFFICIAL TECHNICAL BOOKS

Brooklands Technical Books has been formed to supply owners, restorers and professional repairers

**MG MGA 1500 1600 & 1600 Mk II
OFFICIAL WORKSHOP MANUAL.**
All maintenance and repair procedures.
288 pages, photos, drawings. SB/HB
(AKD600D)

**MG MGA TWIN CAM
OFFICIAL WORKSHOP MANUAL.**
Detailed information on maintaining,
servicing and repair. 240 pages, photos,
drawings. SB (AKD926B)

**MG SERIES MGA 1500
OFFICIAL SERVICE PARTS LIST.**
Complete listing inc. part nos.,
descriptions, modifications, remarks. 270
pages, drawings. SB/HB (AKD1055)

**MG SERIES MGA 1600
OFFICIAL SERVICE PARTS LIST.**
Includes item nos., descriptions, parts
nos., modifications. 352 pages, exploded
drawings. SB/HB. (AKD1215)

**MG MGA
OFFICIAL DRIVER's HANDBOOK.**
Pub. '60. Controls and instruments,
maintenance, servicing. 64 pages,
photos, drawings. SB (AKD598G)

**MG MGA 1600
OFFICIAL DRIVER'S HANDBOOK.**
Pub. '59. All information needed to
maintain the car in satisfactory condition.
64 pages, drawings. SB. (AKD1172)

**MG MGA 1600 MK II
OFFICIAL DRIVER'S HANDBOOK.**
Pub. '61.General data, preparing for the
road, maintenance. 71 pages, drawings.
SB. (AKD195A)

**MG MGA TWIN CAM
OFFICIAL DRIVER'S HANDBOOK.**
Pub. '59. Information on operation and
general maintenance. 64 pages,
drawings. SB. (AKD879)

**MG MGA TWIN CAM
OFFICIAL OWNER'S HANDBOOK.** 3rd
edition. General data, maintenance &
servicing. 64 pages, drawings. SB.
(AKD879B)

Note: SB - soft cover   HB - hard cover

From MG specialists and booksellers or, in case of difficulty, direct from Brooklands Books distributors

BRITISH MOTOR HERITAGE

OFFICIAL TECHNICAL BOOKS

Brooklands Technical Books has been formed to supply owners, restorers and professional repairers with official factory lilterature.

Workshop Manuals

Model	Orig. Part No.
Midget TC (instruction manual)	n/a
Midget TD/TF (SC)	AKD580A
Midget TD/TF (HC)	AKD580A
MG M to TF 1500 (Blower)	XO17
MGA 1500/1600 Mk.2 (SC)	AKD600D
MGA 1500/1600 Mk.2 (HC)	AKD600D
MGA Twin Cam	AKD926B
Midget Mk.1,2 & 3 & Sprite	AKD4021
Midget 1500	AKM4071B
MGB (pub. '76)	AKD3259
MGB GT V8 WSM Supp.	AKD8468
MGC	AKD7133

Parts Catalogues

Model	Orig. Part No.
MGA 1500 (HC)	AKD1055
MGA 1500 (SC)	AKD1055
MGA 1600 & Mk. 2(HC)	AKD1215
MGA 1600 & Mk. 2(SC)	AKD1215
Midget Mk.2 & 3	AKM0036
MGB Tourer GT & V8 (to Sept. '76)	AKM0039
MGB Tourer & GT (Sept. '77)	AKM0037

Owners Handbooks

Model	Orig. Part No.
MG Midget TF & TF 1500	AKM658A
Midget TD	n/a
MGA 1500	AKD598G
MGA 1600	AKD1172
MGA 1600 Mk.2	AKD195A
MGA Twin Cam	AKD879
MGA Twin Cam (3rd edn.)	AKD879B
Midget Mk.3 (pub. '71)	AKD7937
Midget Mk.3 (pub. '73)	AKD7596
Midget Mk.3 (pub. '78)	AKM3229
Midget Mk.3 (pub. '76) (US)	AKM3436
Midget Mk.3 (pub. '79) (US)	AKM4386
MGB Tourer (pub. '65)	AKD3900C
MGB Tourer (pub. '69)	AKD3900J
MGB Tourer & GT (pub.'74)	AKD7598
MGB Tourer (pub. '76)	AKM3661
MG GT V8	AKD8423
MGB (US)(pub. '68)	AKD7059
MGB (US)(pub. '71)	AKD7881
MGB (US)(pub. '73)	AKD8155
MGB (US)(pub. '75)	AKD3286
MGB (US)(pub. '80)	AKM8098
MGB Tourer & GT Tuning	CAKD4034L
MGB Tuning (1800cc)	AKD4034
MGC (pub. '69)	AKD4887B

ALSO AVAILABLE: 180 page 'Glovebox' size owners' workshop manuals:
MGA & MGB & GT 1955-68
MG Sprite & Midget 1, 2, 3, 1500 1958-80
MGB & GT 1968-81

Note: SC - Soft Cover   HC - Hard Cover

From specialist booksellers or, in case of difficulty, direct from the distributors:

Brooklands Books Ltd., PO Box 146, Cobham, Surrey KT11 1LG, England
Phone: 01932 865051   Fax: 01932 868803
Brooklands Books Ltd., 1/81 Darley Street, PO Box 199, Mona Vale, NSW 2103, Australia
Phone: 2 999 78428   Fax: 2 979 5799
Car Tech, 11481 Kost Dam Road, North Branch, MN 55056 USA
Phone: 800 551 4754 & 612 583 3471   Fax: 612 583 2023

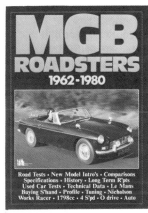

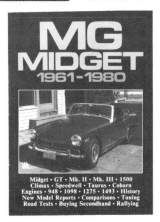
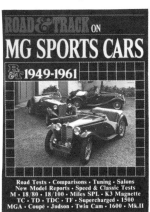
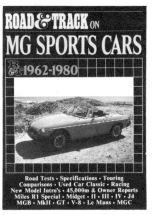

BROOKLANDS BOOKS

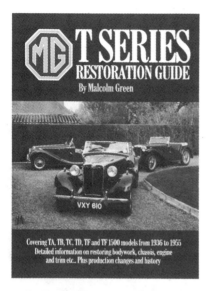

MG T SERIES RESTORATION GUIDE
by Malcolm Green

Detailed information on restoring bodywork, chassis, engine, etc. and supplemented by a good selection of photographs giving both views of work being carried out on the cars and how the completed vehicle should look.

There are tables giving model by model guides to changes in production as well as information on original colour schemes. A step by step guide is given to engine rebuilding, body construction and to trimming the car. 160 large pages, 120 photographs, both colour and black and white, plus many drawings and illustrations.

MGA RESTORATION GUIDE
by Malcolm Green

A book to help owners of these popular sports cars tackle a restoration of their car. There is a chapter giving model by model changes, followed by one giving guidance on looking for a car to restore. Deals with restoration of chassis, steering, suspension, bodywork and replacing rusted panels plus advice on rebuilding pushrod and Twin Cam engines. Step by step guide to trimming with details of period accessories.
160 large pages, 150 photographs, both colour and black and white, plus many drawings and illustrations.

SU CARBURETTERS TUNING TIPS & TECHNIQUES

A comprehensive guide to all SU carburetters and SU fuel pumps - now in its 5th edition. Begins with an explanatory chapter on 'design and function', the book covers all aspects of tuning and repair for the DIY owner and racer, written in easy-to-follow language throughout and illustrated with a helpful variety of charts and exploded drawings.
Ideal companion book for MGA owners. 186 pages

MGA & MGB 1955-1968 OWNERS' WORKSHOP MANUAL

Compact size manual in our 'Glovebox' series. Covering engine, fuel, ignition and cooling systems, plus clutch, gearbox, transmission and suspension. Also deals with steering, braking and electrical systems and bodywork.
Models covered: MGA, MGA 1600, MGA Twin Cam, MGB & MGB GT.
186 pages, well illustrated.

From MG Specialists and booksellers or in case of difficulty direct from Brooklands Book's distributors